52 WEEK Journaling WITH THE Holy Spirit

This journal belongs to

____

52 WEEK Journaling WITH THE Holy Spirit

SCRIPTURES, DEVOTIONS, PRAYERS & PRAISE
TO CONNECT WITH THE SPIRIT OF GOD

Bonnie Rickner Jensen

PARACLETE
PRESS
BREWSTER, MASSACHUSETTS

For my sister, Becky,

who has taught me that full surrender to the Holy Spirit brings the fullest life.

2025 First Printing

Journaling with the Holy Spirit: Scriptures, Devotions, Prayers & Praise to Connect with the Spirit of God

ISBN 979-8-89348-024-5

Library of Congress Control Number: 2025938603

10 9 8 7 6 5 4 3 2 1

Cover design: Paraclete Design
Cover art: Clare Therese Gray

Published by Paraclete Press
Brewster, Massachusetts
www.paracletepress.com

Printed in South Korea

When the Father sends the Comforter instead of me—
and by the Comforter I mean the Holy Spirit—
he will teach you much,
as well as remind you of everything I myself have told you.

—Jesus, as recorded in John 14:26, TLB

CONTENTS

A NOTE FROM THE AUTHOR

Every day, the Spirit of God has something to say to each one of us. Our early waking hours are sacred and pristine—our minds a little less full, our spirits a little more receptive. The evening hours are a time to settle our minds and process the day. Ideally, we carve out a quiet place where our hearts can receive wise and encouraging counsel from the Holy Spirit, our God-given gift. It's a time to pray for His guidance throughout our week. Time with the Spirit is a chance to set ourselves as active listeners to every thought He initiates. This book invites you to listen more keenly, reflect deeply, and respond more quickly. We're individual souls with a collective purpose to love God and one another. Every word the Holy Spirit breathes leads us to a better understanding of how to glorify God and love people the way Jesus did.

Here's to listening well,

Bonnie

ABOUT THIS JOURNAL

Your journal consists of nine different sections:

Scripture

Ponder

Meditate

Guide Me

Teach Me

Reflect

Thanks Be to God

Highlights

Prayer Requests / Answered Prayers

The next few pages will explain these areas in detail so you may get the most out of using your journal and recording your experiences with the Spirit of God!

Scripture

Each week features a new Bible verse as a coloring page. Read and memorize each verse over the course of the week, allowing your heart and mind to absorb the power of God's Word.

Your word is a lamp to my feet and a light to my path.

—Psalm 119:105, NRSVue

Ponder

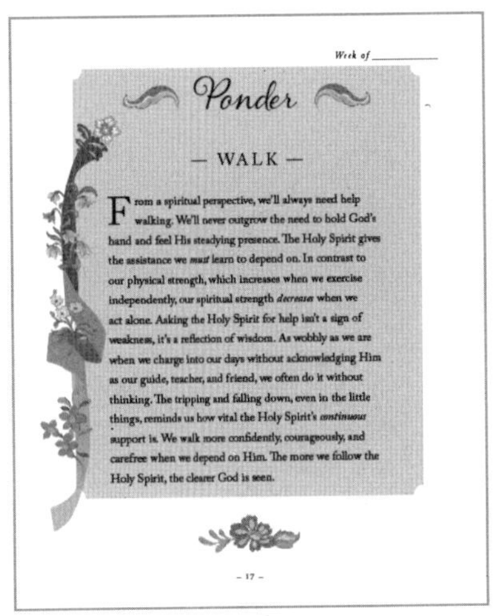

Week of __________

Ponder

— WALK —

From a spiritual perspective, we'll always need help walking. We'll never outgrow the need to hold God's hand and feel His steadying presence. The Holy Spirit gives the assistance we *must* learn to depend on. In contrast to our physical strength, which increases when we exercise independently, our spiritual strength *decreases* when we act alone. Asking the Holy Spirit for help isn't a sign of weakness, it's a reflection of wisdom. As wobbly as we are when we charge into our days without acknowledging Him as our guide, teacher, and friend, we often do it without thinking. The tripping and falling down, even in the little things, reminds us how vital the Holy Spirit's *continuous* support is. We walk more confidently, courageously, and carefree when we depend on Him. The more we follow the Holy Spirit, the clearer God is seen.

– 17 –

What week is it? Record the date and watch how the Holy Spirit moves and speaks to you throughout the year.

Each week includes a short devotion to read and meditate upon, rooted in Scripture. You may use this as an ongoing weekly reflection or fill the space in a single day. Record your response, questions, or other Bible passages that come to mind when reading the entry. Allow your mind to be still and know that He is God. Ask the Holy Spirit to teach you and reveal new insights as you read God's Word.

Be still, and know that I am God!

—Psalm 46:10, NRSVue

Meditate

Read the contemporary message, slow down, and consider how the Holy Spirit might be speaking to your daily walk.

Meditate

To *walk according to the Spirit* means to *depend on the Holy Spirit* every day with consistency. The late Andrew Murray, church leader and missionary statesman, wrote, "Acknowledge that you have grieved the Holy Spirit by your self-will, self-confidence, and self-effort." Humility in prayer is the way to start our day, inviting the Spirit of God to be involved in *everything* we do. He will be faithful in the task.

Guide Me

Teach Me

Guide Me

We depend on the Holy Spirit to continuously guide us. What specific decisions and circumstances need His guidance this week?

Teach Me

In which areas of your life might the Holy Spirit teach you more about God's character, the fruit of the Spirit, or the lens of worshipful living?

For just as the heavens are higher than the earth, so are my ways higher than yours, and my thoughts than yours.

—Isaiah 55:9, TLB

Reflect

And I will ask the Father, and he will give you another advocate to help you and be with you forever—the Spirit of truth. The world cannot accept him, because it neither sees him nor knows him. But you know him, for he lives with you and will be in you.

—John 14:16–17, NIV

Reflect

Is there a recent time you've seen the direct intervention of the Holy Spirit in a choice you've made?

In contrast, is there a decision you've made without *the direction of the Holy Spirit that allowed Him to teach you wisdom going forward?*

How can you best practice the daily discipline of inviting the Holy Spirit into your thoughts and actions?

Thanks Be to God

Highlights

– 19 –

Each week includes a special reflection verse that is different from the coloring page verse to accentuate the Spirit of God living and breathing throughout the Old Testament, New Testament, and your life today.

Read each prompt and record your answers throughout each week.

Thanks Be to God

What are you thankful for this week? Praise Father, Son, and Holy Spirit for blessings in your life.

Highlights

Take time to write down a few "highlights" of listening to and following the Holy Spirit in your walk with Him this week.

And I am sure that God who began the good work within you will keep right on helping you grow in his grace until his task within you is finally finished on that day when Jesus Christ returns.

—Philippians 1:6, TLB

Prayer Requests / Answered Prayers

Record your prayers. Write them down as the year progresses and seek the Holy Spirit to intercede on your behalf.

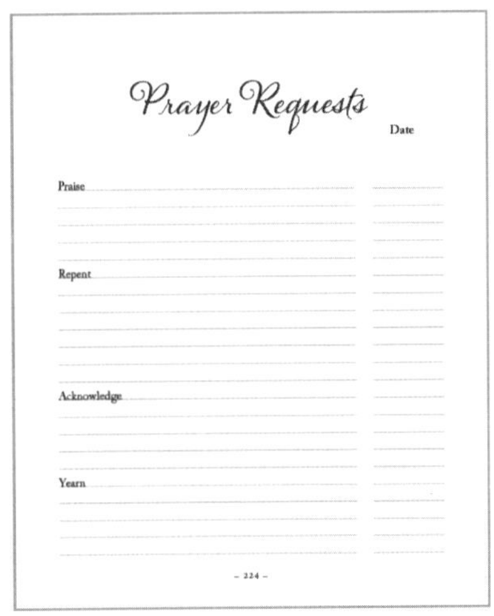
Prayer Requests
Date
Praise
Repent
Acknowledge
Yearn
– 224 –

Record the date you began praying about your request and the date the prayer is answered.

Be mindful of how the Holy Spirit moves with you and how your prayers are answered. Trust in God's timing and His plans for working all things together for your good.

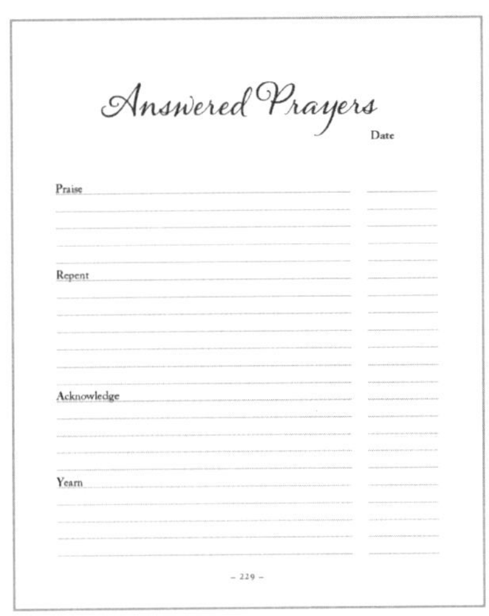
Answered Prayers
Date
Praise
Repent
Acknowledge
Yearn
– 229 –

And in the same way—by our faith—the Holy Spirit helps us with our daily problems and in our praying. For we don't even know what we should pray for nor how to pray as we should, but the Holy Spirit prays for us with such feeling that it cannot be expressed in words.

—Romans 8:26, TLB

There is therefore now no condemnation
to those who are in Christ Jesus,
who do not walk according to the flesh,
but according to the Spirit.
—*Romans 8:1, NKJV*

Ponder

— WALK —

From a spiritual perspective, we'll always need help walking. We'll never outgrow the need to hold God's hand and feel His steadying presence. The Holy Spirit gives the assistance we *must* learn to depend on. In contrast to our physical strength, which increases when we exercise independently, our spiritual strength *decreases* when we act alone. Asking the Holy Spirit for help isn't a sign of weakness, it's a reflection of wisdom. As wobbly as we are when we charge into our days without acknowledging Him as our guide, teacher, and friend, we often do it without thinking. The tripping and falling down, even in the little things, reminds us how vital the Holy Spirit's *continuous* support is. We walk more confidently, courageously, and carefree when we depend on Him. The more we follow the Holy Spirit, the clearer God is seen.

Meditate

To *walk according to the Spirit* means to *depend on the Holy Spirit* every day with consistency. The late Andrew Murray, church leader and missionary statesman, wrote, "Acknowledge that you have grieved the Holy Spirit by your self-will, self-confidence, and self-effort." Humility in prayer is the way to start our day, inviting the Spirit of God to be involved in *everything* we do. He will be faithful in the task.

Guide Me

Teach Me

And I will ask the Father, and he will give you another advocate to help you and be with you forever—the Spirit of truth. The world cannot accept him, because it neither sees him nor knows him. But you know him, for he lives with you and will be in you.

—John 14:16–17, NIV

Reflect

Is there a recent time you've seen the direct intervention of the Holy Spirit in a choice you've made?

In contrast, is there a decision you've made without *the direction of the Holy Spirit that allowed Him to teach you wisdom going forward?*

How can you best practice the daily discipline of inviting the Holy Spirit into your thoughts and actions?

Thanks Be to God

Highlights

Don't hide your light! Let it shine for all;
let your good deeds glow for all to see,
so that they will praise your heavenly Father.
—Matthew 5:15–16, TLB

Ponder

— GLOW —

The Holy Spirit will always echo the words of Jesus. What our Savior taught His disciples while on this earth, the Holy Spirit repeats to us today. When we feel discouraged and the light of our life dims, we can depend on the Holy Spirit to illuminate the truth: *In the world you will have tribulation; but be of good cheer, Jesus has overcome the world* (see John 16:33). Overcoming looks and feels different than it did when Jesus was here, but our victory over *whatever* comes against us is no less sure. With the Holy Spirit beside us, we are never void of the power of God. There isn't a moment's interruption in its flow. Our authority is in remembering, reciting, and rejoicing in the truth God has given us. The more we rely on the Holy Spirit, the louder His voice becomes in our thought life, our prayer life, and our daily decision-making. He is a *constant* friend—*especially* when we need comfort and encouragement to ignite the light of truth within us.

Meditate

What a humbling thing for God's servant Daniel to hear from a king: *"I have heard of you, that the Spirit of God is in you."* Our first priority in letting the light of God shine out from us is knowing the truth. For the Holy Spirit to show the Word of God shining through us, we need the Word of God living in us. The Spirit of God cannot bring to our remembrance the teaching of Jesus if He cannot draw from a well of truth we've deposited in our hearts.God has given us an endless supply. It's up to us to keep our souls filled.

Guide Me

Teach Me

I have heard of you, that the Spirit of God is in you, and that light and understanding and excellent wisdom are found in you.

—Daniel 5:14, NKJV

Reflect

Do you remember the hope you felt the first time the light of Jesus shined on you?

What ignites your desire to be a reflection of God's light in the world?

The Holy Spirit is here to remind you of the power that's in the divine glow of your life.

In what specific area is He asking you to illuminate the lives of those around you?

Thanks Be to God

Highlights

Wait on the Lord; Be of good courage,
And He shall strengthen your heart;
Wait, I say, on the Lord!
—Psalm 27:14, NKJV

Ponder

— WAIT —

The enemy of our soul wants us to give up waiting on God, because God's plan for our lives is perfect—and perfectly timed. The presence of the Holy Spirit brings an unquenchable hope in the valleys of life. We all go through trials, and we *get* through them courageously with the companionship of the Holy Spirit. The apostle Paul prayed in Romans 15:13, *"May the God of hope fill you with all joy and peace in believing, that you may abound in hope by the power of the Holy Spirit"* (NKJV). Giving up short circuits God's best, and sends our minds into a sea of hopelessness and our bodies into a state of stress. This is when we ask the Holy Spirit to fill our minds with *truth*. We have a future and a hope (Jeremiah 29:11). Our steps are directed (Proverbs 16:9). God will never leave or forsake us (Deuteronomy 31:6). God can be trusted, *always* (Psalm 9:10). The temptation to become impatient with God is no new thing, no groundbreaking tactic. The plan is as old as time and as tired as the enemy's creativity. Abounding in hope isn't always easy—but by the power of the Holy Spirit, it is always within a prayer's reach.

Meditate

In our human strength, we're easily discouraged and distracted. While waiting for God to answer in our time of need or to fulfill the desires of our heart, we subconsciously put time limits on the expected results. We become distracted by attempts to work things out on our own. Putting ourselves ahead of God displaces the Holy Spirit. He is our gift, our friend, our teacher, and our first line of defense in seeing every promise God has given come to fruition in our lives.

Guide Me

Teach Me

They that wait upon the Lord shall renew their strength. They shall mount up with wings like eagles; they shall run and not be weary; they shall walk and not faint.
—Isaiah 40:31, TLB

Reflect

Do you trust God's timing without hesitation?

How can you resist the desire to bypass the counsel and comfort of the Holy Spirit while waiting for God's answer?

What is a foundational Scripture you go to in order to resist the enemy's attempt to steal your hope?

Thanks Be to God

Highlights

Pray without ceasing.

—1 Thessalonians 5:17, NKJV

Week of: ____________

Ponder

— SPEAK —

Prayer is power—a power nothing on Earth can match and nothing in Heaven can ignore. We have a prayer partner in the Holy Spirit, One who is always by our side. Our prayers are in full agreement with His when we speak the Word of God. Not only do we garner the power of His agreement, but also we gather the support of the heavenly host. *Bless the LORD, you His angels, Who excel in strength, who do His word, heeding the voice of His word* (Psalm 103:20, NKJV). The angels *hear* and *do*. The Holy Spirit calls to our remembrance what God says and what Jesus has done. Everything we need in this life is fully ours by the finished work of our faithful Savior. There's no ally more certain of that than the Holy Spirit, the One who stands with us, believes with us, and prays with us. Not a single part of the Trinity's equation can fail. The Father, the Son, and the Holy Spirit are faithful to every promise God has given. When truth fills our minds and hearts, we can speak it confidently, knowing that giving it voice moves the angels to action.

Meditate

There are times when we pray in our hearts like Hannah did. *Now Hannah spoke in her heart; only her lips moved, but her voice was not heard* (1 Samuel 1:13a, NKJV). At other times, we need to speak the Word of God, which is *living and powerful* (Hebrews 4:12, NKJV). It *sets in motion* the heavenly host, who *heed the voice of God's Word* (see Psalm 103:20). *Heed* means to pay close attention and to take action. There's something powerful about releasing the *living Word* into the air around us. Sound waves create vibration, and movement draws attention. God the Father is *always* paying attention—as are the Holy Spirit, our Savior, and the angels in God's command. When we *speak* the Word, we *activate* its power—in our life and into our circumstances, for the purpose of initiating the desired change.

Guide Me

Teach Me

Take the helmet of salvation, and the sword of the Spirit, which is the word of God; praying always with all prayer and supplication in the Spirit.

—Ephesians 6:17–18a, NKJV

Reflect

How often do you pray out loud?

Do you feel it makes a difference to hear yourself speaking the living and powerful Word of God?

In Ephesians 6:17, RHEMA, the Greek word Paul uses for the "Word of God," means "utterance"—which changes the reading to, "the sword of the Spirit is the spoken Word of God." How might this change your prayer life?

Thanks Be to God

Highlights

And we know that all things work together for good
to those who love God, to those who are the called
according to His purpose.
—Romans 8:28, NKJV

Ponder

— TRUST —

Where we are in our lives, what we're doing, and who we're affecting, are a valuable part of our journey. The Holy Spirit, our constant companion, sees each of us from every perspective—most importantly, from God's point of view. Even though we don't make all the right choices along the way, God is *actively* involved at all times. When we lose sight or get off track, the Holy Spirit is an infallible guide for each hard-fought, sometimes painful step that leads us back to the perfect will of God. Jesus, the Author of our stories, uses every step to draw us closer to Him. As a loving Father, God uses every choice as a catalyst for our spiritual growth. The closer we are to the Holy Spirit, the deeper we understand the grace of our Savior and the joy of being close to God. Nothing is more fulfilling. Our missteps aren't too great to be forgiven, and our mistakes won't escape God's mercy. *Though your sins are like scarlet, They shall be as white as snow* (Isaiah 1:18, NKJV). God is unflinchingly faithful. When our trust level goes up, the peace of God reaches in, keeping our hearts and minds certain that He'll use *every* step of our journey for our good and His glory.

Meditate

We know life isn't a continuous series of good events and comfortable circumstances. There are tests and trials of various kinds (James 1:2–4). Living surrendered to God and dependent on the Holy Spirit is the only way to see everything from a divine perspective. What happens to us must go through God first, and we can trust that with absolute certainty. Part of the gift of the Holy Spirit is the promise to teach us. In the midst of our trials, when we have more questions than answers, the Holy Spirit will show us how God intends to grow us. We're in the palm of our loving Father's hand, and *every* outcome is part of His plan.

Guide Me

Teach Me

They cried out to God in the battle.
He heeded their prayer, because they put their trust in Him.
—1 Chronicles 5:20b, NKJV

Reflect

What trust-building trial have you gone through recently?

What did the Holy Spirit teach you, and how did your absolute trust in God grow in the process?

As for God, His way is perfect; The word of the LORD is proven; He is a shield to all who trust in Him (Psalm 18:30, NKJV). God's way is perfect in a world that's broken. Is it difficult for you to trust God without question?

Thanks Be to God

Highlights

Teach me to do Your will, for You are my God;
Your Spirit is good.
—Psalm 143:10, NKJV

Ponder

— SURRENDER —

Through prayer, we can draw an abiding comfort from the Holy Spirit that keeps fear from settling in our hearts and minds. Fear and suffering create a void only God can fill. The Holy Spirit was sent to be our Comforter in this life. When we surrender to God, lean on the Holy Spirit, and fall into the depths of our Savior's compassion, our brokenness becomes a divine battlefield. The Holy Trinity fights for us in our helplessness and lifts our burdens. They carry us away from the war-torn places in our souls and renew our strength. At the point where we surrender fully to the will of God and the overcoming power of Jesus, the indwelling, sustaining presence of the Holy Spirit conquers fear, because we know our Comforter is near. With complete surrender comes enduring calm, forcing every fear to fold beneath the power of God's love.

Meditate

It takes resolve to *completely abandon* our own ways and our own ideas of how God should conduct our lives. We're human, and to a very real extent, we want to be in control. That feels safer, we decide. That feels responsible, we determine. Commanding control of our lives is essentially putting a gift from God on the shelf. What good can come from declining a gift from God? The Holy Spirit is a gift that *abides* with us. Involving Him in every decision we make shows wisdom. Being an active listener reflects a surrendered heart and a willing obedience to God's Word.

Guide Me

Teach Me

Fear not, for I am with you. Do not be dismayed. I am your God.
I will strengthen you; I will help you;
I will uphold you with my victorious right hand.
—Isaiah 41:10, TLB

Reflect

What area of your life is the hardest to surrender to the guidance of the Holy Spirit?

The Holy Spirit is a gift through which God's power is continuously given to us. Do you practice a keen awareness of His active presence with you at all times?

Surrendering every decision to God's will is possible by listening to the Holy Spirit. How often do you submit to His leading at the beginning of your day?

Thanks Be to God

Highlights

Hear my prayer, O Lord, And give ear to my cry;
Do not be silent at my tears.
—Psalm 39:12a, NKJV

Ponder

— CRY —

We're able to face some of our days with a firm, confident grip on grace. On other days, we're swimming in the emotion of our challenges and circumstances. We can't help breaking down—but a good cry is never a bad idea. Not only does the Holy Spirit understand, but He's also here to remind us that Jesus empathizes with everything we go through from His own human experience. *For we do not have a High Priest who cannot sympathize with our weaknesses, but was in all points tempted as we are, yet without sin. Let us therefore come boldly to the throne of grace, that we may obtain mercy and find grace to help in the time of need* (Hebrews 4:15–16, NKJV). There's a raw honesty that surfaces when our tears flow. Tears can be a spillover from the stresses we don't surrender to God's care. Tears can be a release from swells of grief, unexpected tragedy, or ongoing trials. But crying often accompanies our most transparent conversations with God. Our defenses wash away, our weaknesses lie bare, and our desperate need for the solace of the Holy Spirit emerges. When our tears flow, our hearts know we can't do this life without going boldly to the throne of grace in our time of need—and that's a *very* good place to be.

Meditate

You have collected all my tears and preserved them in your bottle (Psalm 56:8, TLB). What a beautiful image of God's compassion. The pain we suffer is part of the story of our lives. Often, the lowest times are intimate moments no one knows about except our triune God, as He holds our grief-split hearts together. This supernatural team—our compassionate Father, our loving Savior, and our faithful Comforter—carries us through our darkest hours without fail.

Guide Me

Teach Me

You have seen me tossing and turning throughout the night. You have collected all my tears and preserved them in your bottle! You have recorded every one in your book.

—Psalm 56:8, TLB

Reflect

Do you go to God first at your most vulnerable times?

Solitude encourages conversations with the Holy Spirit. Are you making enough time for yourself when you need His comfort?

Being transparent with God in prayer helps to heal us. He sees our hearts and understands our pains, but He knows that pouring them out is good for us. How often do you empty your heart to God?

Thanks Be to God

Highlights

The believers learned how to walk in the fear of the Lord
and in the comfort of the Holy Spirit.
—Acts 9:31b, TLB

Ponder

— BREATHE —

The world is full of temptations to keep us worn out physically, emotionally, and spiritually. We sprint through our days to prove our worth at home, at work, as friends, and on social media. The ongoing pressure to be the best we can be in every area of our lives can leave us feeling out of breath. Thankfully, the Holy Spirit is the air we need. God sent Him to help us in this race, to be the oxygen that keeps every part of our being healthy, strong, and wise. *Let us lay aside every weight, and the sin which so easily ensnares us, and let us run with endurance the race that is set before us* (Hebrews 12:1, NKJV). When we feel too tired to go on, it's because we too often fail to acknowledge the gift of the Holy Spirit as our constant, ready help. Asking Him to get involved in everything we do takes the pressure off and sets our priorities straight. Ignoring Him saps our strength, while paying attention to His steadying presence allows us to breathe with ease. The Holy Spirit is a friend whose focus is our well-being—so we can run our race of faith, learn to love like Jesus, and live for the glory of God.

Meditate

Learning how to walk in submission to God with the support of the Holy Spirit leads to the abundant life Jesus came to give. Living at a fever pitch, bearing the weight of our days, and striving to maintain a balance will only lead to an unfulfilled, exhausted life. The Holy Spirit is here to be the weight bearer, the friend, and the one who keeps us in the center of God's will. Trusting Him throughout our days, in all things big and small, is how we learn to walk in the comfort of His teaching, wisdom, and peace.

Guide Me

Teach Me

He [Jesus] spoke to them again and said, "As the Father has sent me, even so I am sending you." Then he breathed on them and told them, "Receive the Holy Spirit."
—*John 20:21–22, TLB*

Reflect

How quickly do you ask for the Holy Spirit's input when faced with a decision?

It's vital to our victory as children of God to let the peace of the Holy Spirit rule our life. Learning to walk closely with Him frees us to live with a fearless confidence in God. Are you aware of and listening for the guiding truth He brings to your remembrance?

The Holy Spirit leads by peace. How do you pause to let your spirit exhale and submit to His leading throughout your day?

Thanks Be to God

Highlights

If you want to know what God wants you to do, ask him,
and he will gladly tell you, for he is always ready
to give a bountiful supply of wisdom to all who ask him.
—James 1:5, TLB

Ponder

— SEEK —

It's up to us—and for our *greatest* benefit—to shorten the amount of time it takes to seek the counsel of the Holy Spirit about the course of our day. It's a prayerful habit we should initiate when we open our eyes every morning. We don't have moments to waste when it comes to tapping into the divine and loving wisdom available to us. Letting time pass before we ask for the guidance of the Holy Spirit prolongs the outcomes that please God and align with His Word. When we plow through our days without praying, seeking, asking, and listening, we tax our emotional energy and weaken our spiritual strength. The Father's hope is that our relationship with the Holy Spirit is one of *constant* camaraderie: *a mutual friendship between those who spend a lot of time together.* Time spent seeking leads to less time struggling with the decisions that are wisest and the direction that is best.

Meditate

It can seem the world is growing darker by the day, with fewer recognizing the truth while leveling more assaults against it. The Holy Spirit has never been more important to the health of our spirit and the hope of our calling. What God has freely given us is the grace to love others the way He does, with the consistent, compassionate help of the Holy Spirit. Those who haven't received the Spirit of God don't understand the truth we walk in, the hope that sustains us, or the wisdom we depend on. What they do understand is love in action, which inspires them to seek the One we serve.

Guide Me

Teach Me

No one knows the things of God except the Spirit of God. Now we have received, not the spirit of the world, but the Spirit who is from God, that we might know the things that have been freely given to us by God.

—1 Corinthians 2:11–12, NKJV

Reflect

Seeking a greater dependence on the Holy Spirit comes with knowing God's Word in great depth. The will of God is what the Holy Spirit wants for us. Do you consistently set aside time to fill your heart and mind with truth?

When we seek to know God more, we desire a deeper relationship with the Holy Spirit. Have you discovered a sweeter dependence on Him?

How has the Holy Spirit deepened your knowledge of God's Word throughout this week?

Thanks Be to God

Highlights

Teach us to number our days,
That we may gain a heart of wisdom.
—Psalm 90:12, NKJV

Ponder

— GAIN —

Gaining confidence in the Holy Spirit comes when we *continuously* tap into the purpose God had for sending Him. He's here to remind us of the truth Jesus spoke, to teach us things we don't yet know, and to show us things we need to see. Listening requires our deliberate attention to the Holy Spirit's presence. We render Him silent by ignoring Him. If we ask, there's no waiting for an answer—the Holy Spirit is given to us as a powerful, prepared, and present friend. It's as simple as whispering a prayer and trusting our responses to His lead. Learning to be receptive to the Holy Spirit takes practice and obedience. If we pause and listen before we act or react, it won't take long to realize the reward of the right responses He gives. They always promote peace, they always convey love, and they *always* honor God.

Meditate

To gain anything in life, physically or spiritually, we must apply ourselves. Gaining a daily, continual confidence in the Holy Spirit mandates three things: our reception of the gift that the Holy Spirit is, our respect for His oneness with the Father, and our obedience to the teaching of Jesus that He faithfully recalls to us. The Holy Spirit is our gateway to gaining wisdom, garnering peace, and glorifying God.

Guide Me

Teach Me

Fix your attention on God. You'll be changed from the inside out. Readily recognize what he wants from you, and quickly respond to it. Unlike the culture around you, always dragging you down to its level of immaturity, God brings the best out of you, develops well-formed maturity in you.

—Romans 12:2, MSG

Reflect

Our personality traits make our challenges unique. What parts of your life are most challenging when it comes to growing your confidence in the Holy Spirit?

Changing from the inside out requires an unwavering focus on God. What distracts you most often? Are there areas in which you trust yourself too quickly without the Holy Spirit's inclusion?

If you gained a confidence in the Holy Spirit that resulted in more peace and less stress, how would this improve your life?

Thanks Be to God

Highlights

Grow in spiritual strength
and become better acquainted
with our Lord and Savior Jesus Christ.
—2 Peter 3:18a, TLB

Ponder

— GROW —

The Holy Spirit is our *present* help. When we reflect on the past, the Holy Spirit puts a spotlight on God's faithfulness. He will never fill our minds with regret, replay our mistakes, or remind us of the wrong choices we've made. God's mercy rises with the sun and heralds hope—and that's where the Spirit of God dwells. Every complaint serves as a setback. Self-talk that leads to self-pity becomes a stumbling block. The Holy Spirit is with us today to promote our *growth*. The day swells with opportunities to practice love without judgment or expectations. God's love for us is our blueprint for loving others, and the Holy Spirit is our faithful teacher. Listening is learned by quiet practice. Alone, we're able to hear best. In silent prayer, we invite the insightful, encouraging leadership of the Holy Spirit. He's our closest friend and wisest counsel. He's our deep, divine Comforter. He's the difference-maker in the course of *every* day. When the Holy Spirit has control, God has our surrender. That's a place where God's power can work in miraculous ways.

Meditate

Growing in trust and wisdom means going forward. The only thing from our past that should follow us into our present and future is what the Holy Spirit has taught us. Seasons of growth often happen during times of spiritual wilderness, when it feels like God is silent and the Holy Spirit is asleep. Neither is *ever* true. Growing in spiritual strength takes trust and patience. The Holy Spirit reveals what God is doing for our good and His glory when it will most shape our hearts. We see, in perfect timing, how God uses circumstances, experiences, and trials to draw us closer to Him—and how *nothing* in this world is more fulfilling.

Guide Me

Teach Me

When the Holy Spirit, who is the truth, comes, he shall guide you into all truth, for he will not be presenting his own ideas, but will be passing on to you what he has heard. He will tell you about the future.

—John 16:13, TLB

Reflect

How has God used your circumstances to grow your spiritual strength?

What is the single most impactful life experience you've gone through that has deepened your faith?

Has the Holy Spirit shown you something this week revealing God's active work in your life?

Thanks Be to God

Highlights

A relaxed attitude lengthens a man's life.
—Proverbs 14:30a, TLB

Week of: ___________

Ponder

— RELAX —

A quiet, hopeful, ongoing surrender to the Holy Spirit is a powerful, ready weapon in a life of faith. Surrendering to the constant care of our loving Father is the only way to relinquish control and live unburdened. Every burden we carry, even in the far reaches of our mind, creates a pool of tension that fuels anxiety. Without realizing it, strongholds build up in our subconscious and threaten our peace and ability to stay calm. The Holy Spirit is the best stress diffuser we have. Giving control to Him at daybreak, as soon as we open our eyes, helps empty out anything unlike God that might be hidden within us. God didn't create our minds to be holding tanks for things He promises to take care of—which is *everything* we need. He's got it all covered, so we can be busy loving one another and being kind, serving selflessly and giving generously, forgiving freely and fostering unity. When we pray for every thought, word, and action to be guided by the Holy Spirit, we allow God to influence our actions with love and grace. We're able to fully relax and let God move through us, into a world that so desperately needs Him.

Meditate

A calm, relaxed attitude is undervalued in the world today. Keeping anxiety at bay and maintaining a state of calmness isn't easy in our fast-paced lives. Without a dependence on the Holy Spirit, we have no chance of achieving it. The world offers many helpful solutions. But our victory comes by realizing, keenly and in every moment, that we have the Spirit of God *in residence.* Our body houses more power than we can comprehend against every fear, doubt, and peace-threatening weapon in the enemy's arsenal. The Holy Spirit is our friend for the win—and all the promises of God are with Him.

Guide Me

Teach Me

God the Father chose you long ago and knew you would become his children. And the Holy Spirit has been at work in your hearts, cleansing you with the blood of Jesus Christ and making you to please him. May God bless you richly and grant you increasing freedom from all anxiety and fear.

—1 Peter 1:2, TLB

Reflect

What encourages you to relax and let go of burdens, competition, or resentments you've tried to carry?

Asking the Holy Spirit to help us surrender control to God is a first step to eliminating hidden stress. Do you depend on the Holy Spirit to calm you throughout the day?

The act of relaxing ushers in peace, which welcomes the Holy Spirit into our hearts and minds. Are you intentional about carving out time to relax?

Thanks Be to God

Highlights

Be still, and know that I am God.
—Psalm 46:10, NKJV

Ponder

— KNOW —

Beyond a shadow of a doubt, without a single question, and no matter how high the odds are stacked against us, we *know* God is for us and His gifts are good. The Holy Spirit is a good gift in every way imaginable. The battles we fight begin in our mind and influence our physical, emotional, and spiritual well-being. Our sure win depends on keeping the right thoughts in play in order to keep the wrong ones silenced. When *You can't do this* comes to mind, *I can do all things through Christ who strengthens me* is our answer (Philippians 4:13, NKJV). When *This scares me* rings loud, *God has not given us a spirit of fear, but of power, and of love and of a sound mind* is our defense (2 Timothy 1:7, NKJV). For every thought filled with fear and doubt, God has a response filled with faith and hope—and the Holy Spirit is His megaphone. He knows every truth and every spiritual weapon at our disposal, and He knows exactly which one to put in our hand.

Meditate

"Be still and know again what I've done for you." That's what God instructs us to do when we feel embattled by worry, frustration, or mental exhaustion. In other words, God wants us to put His goodness on repeat. He's been faithful in the past, He's faithful in the present, and He'll be faithful until we take our last breath. The Holy Spirit is our faithful reminder of truth: *All those who know your mercy, Lord, will count on you for help. For you have never yet forsaken those who trust in you* (Psalm 9:10, TLB); *The very day I call for help, the tide of battle turns. . . . This one thing I know: God is for me!* (Psalm 56:9, TLB). With our minds focused on truth, we know God is handling every part of our life with a love greater than we can comprehend.

Guide Me

Teach Me

If God is for us, who can be against us? He who did not spare His own Son, but delivered Him up for us all, how shall He not with Him also freely give us all things?
—Romans 8:31–32, NKJV

Reflect

How has God come through for you in a tough situation, giving you confidence in knowing He'll do it again?

God is on your side and for you at all times. How does this truth affect you when things in your life don't go as planned?

The Holy Spirit reveals things to increase our understanding and give us wisdom in God's ways. What has He shown you during a time of testing or on the other side of a trial?

Thanks Be to God

Highlights

Patience develops strength of character
in us and helps us trust God more each time we use it
until finally our hope and faith are
strong and steady.
—Romans 5:4, TLB

Ponder

— PREPARE —

The Holy Spirit knows the great purpose He has in reminding us of the words Jesus spoke to His disciples. Knowing what Jesus taught prepares us to handle the storms of life and be wise to the schemes of the enemy. Praying the truth releases the power of God's Word to overcome anything that comes against us. Truth is the foundation of our *best* life. God has given us the way, now it's up to us to wield the power. It's a power the Holy Spirit brings when we accept Jesus as Savior. From that point forward, the name of Jesus sounds the spiritual alarm. All He did to overcome the world becomes the weapon we possess. *Nothing*—on Earth or in Heaven—can defeat it. When we say "Jesus" often enough, we pave a path to victory in every area. The Holy Spirit puts the hope in our hearts, the power of Jesus puts the victory in our hands, and the glory of God puts the praise in our mouths.

Meditate

The apostle Paul's prayer for Christians is that God, the giver of hope, keeps us happy and full of peace as we believe in Him. The second part of Paul's prayer is that God will help us *overflow with hope* through the power of the Helper whom God sent to us—the Holy Spirit. We have *within* us all the hope-sustaining strength we will ever need. When we feel it slipping, the Holy Spirit is our help, our comforter, and the friend who has the power to turn our eyes upward. *Be merciful, O Lord, for I am looking up to you in constant hope* (Psalm 86:3, TLB).

Guide Me

Teach Me

So I pray for you Gentiles that God who gives you hope will keep you happy and full of peace as you believe in him. I pray that God will help you overflow with hope in him through the Holy Spirit's power within you.

—Romans 15:13, TLB

Reflect

How do you keep your hope from fading in the face of disappointment or rejection?

The Holy Spirit's power within us sustains hope in every promise God has made. In what ways do you tap into that power to stay positive and hopeful?

The Holy Spirit encourages us through God's Word. What Bible verses give you hope when you feel down? Write them in your journal this week and say them aloud often.

Thanks Be to God

Highlights

Ask, and it will be given to you;
seek, and you will find; knock,
and it will be opened to you.
—Matthew 7:7, NKJV

Ponder

— PERSIST —

Persistence is a necessary discipline in a life of faith. When we're going through a season of waiting, the testing of our faith can wear down the persistence of our hope. The Holy Spirit is here to push us forward. There will be days when everything falls into question—our trust in God's choices for us, our comprehension of God's grace, the effectiveness of our prayers in light of God's promises. Yet we *persist*. The Holy Spirit is at the ready to instill us with courage. We will persist, knowing God *will not* leave us in a field of unfulfilled promises. However long the trial, the persistence of our faith is building a long list of reasons to be thankful and a longer list of reasons to pray. *One day Jesus told his disciples a story to illustrate their need for constant prayer and to show them that they must keep praying until the answer comes* (Luke 18:1, TLB). We must *persist*. We must *keep asking*. Most importantly, we must *count on the Holy Spirit* to renew our hope in God's faithfulness. The answer is coming.

Meditate

It's tempting to give up when disappointments mount, the wait is long, and we wonder—almost daily—how long it will take for patience to have its perfect work. *Count it all joy when you fall into various trials, knowing that the testing of your faith produces patience. But let patience have its perfect work, that you may be perfect and complete, lacking nothing* (James 1:2–4, NKJV). The Holy Spirit knows the time and distance, and He knows God's love is gauging it. Our hope holds by His constant presence and power.

Guide Me

Teach Me

"Not by might nor by power, but by My Spirit," Says the Lord of hosts.
—Zechariah 4:6, NKJV

Reflect

Remaining steadfast, or firmly fixed in place, takes unfaltering dependence on the Holy Spirit. We might feel wobbly, but the Spirit will not waver. How consistent is your communication with Him when you feel spiritually tired?

When faith is being tested, patience can experience a growth spurt. How have the challenges you've gone through made you more patient and reliant on the Ancient of Days?

Persistence takes some grit on our part. We have to dig in our heels and refuse to give up on God's wisdom. What has helped you hold fast in a time of waiting?

Thanks Be to God

Highlights

Now this is the confidence that we have in Him,
that if we ask anything according to His will,
He hears us.
—1 John 5:14, NKJV

Ponder

— ASK —

When Jesus taught His disciples how to pray, He told them not to pray openly for the sake of being seen. He instructed them not to use vain repetitions like an unbeliever would—reciting words that are rehearsed and void of faith. Jesus said, *Therefore do not be like them. For your Father knows the things you have need of before you ask Him* (Matthew 6:8, NKJV). God knows what we need. He knows every hope, dream, and desire in between, too. But Jesus wasn't telling us not to ask the Father for gifts. The Holy Spirit is a gift. A breathtaking sunrise and a walk on the beach are gifts. A job we love is a gift. Every child is a gift. Jesus was helping the disciples understand that they don't need to talk to God about what's in their hearts out loud and in the streets. *But you, when you pray, go into your room, and when you have shut your door, pray to your Father who is in the secret place; and your Father who sees in secret will reward you openly* (Matthew 6:6, NKJV). Because we have a compassionate Father, asking God for things we want and hope for is a welcome request—and without a doubt, we can expect His best.

Meditate

Solomon became king at a young age and asked God for wisdom to be a good leader. In response, God gave him more wisdom than anyone on earth, then added what he didn't ask for—honor and riches beyond his imagination. If we are in harmony with the Holy Spirit, what we ask God for will embody the same humility. We will ask for self-control when we're angry, so our words hold grace and not harm. We will ask for hearts that love generously and give selflessly. We will ask God to open our eyes to every need in front of us and to bless us with the ability to meet each need. All that we ask—enveloped in humility and bound by faith—will be received by our loving Father and be answered in endless measure.

Guide Me

Teach Me

If you then, being evil, know how to give good gifts to your children, how much more will your heavenly Father give the Holy Spirit to those who ask Him!
—Luke 11:13, NKJV

Reflect

Is there a spiritual discipline you've asked God to help you initiate or maintain?

What area—emotionally or spiritually—do you need to ask the Holy Spirit to help you with?

If you knew it would be given immediately, what would you ask God for today?

Thanks Be to God

Highlights

Without faith it is impossible to please Him,
for he who comes to God must believe that He is,
and that He is a rewarder of those
who diligently seek Him.
—Hebrews 11:6, NKJV

Ponder

— BELIEVE —

How does the world identify you as a child of God? Without a word spoken or exchanged, our lives should reflect the character of God through the Holy Spirit within us. *The fruit of the Spirit is love, joy, peace, longsuffering, kindness, goodness, faithfulness, gentleness, and self-control* (Galatians 5:22–23, NKJV). The moment we believe in Jesus Christ as Lord, the Holy Spirit moves in with the transforming power of God. We who believe without seeing are even more blessed than those who saw our resurrected Lord. Jesus told a doubting Thomas, *Because you have seen Me, you have believed. Blessed are those who have not seen and yet have believed* (John 20:29, NKJV). As we mature in Christ and develop a close-knit relationship with the Holy Spirit, it seems impossible to *not* believe, even though we haven't seen Jesus face-to-face. As we let the Holy Spirit guide us every day, and learn how much He cares about every detail of our lives, there's no doubting the gift we've been given. We believe God sent the Holy Spirit, we believe He's our friend, comforter, helper, and teacher. We believe that staying in God's good and perfect will depends on our close and thriving relationship with the Holy Spirit—and it's a relationship worth investing in every day.

Meditate

Worshipping and pleasing God is a priority when the Holy Spirit is in control. When we believe we have everything we need to live an abundant life through the power of the Holy Spirit, *all* our desires and the actions that follow align with the will of God. Believing in God's love toward us *never* changes through the growing process. This faith keeps our hearts passionate about diligently seeking Him; seeking Him for the purpose of serving Him is our greatest, most fulfilling reward.

Guide Me

Teach Me

When you believed in Christ, he identified you as his own by giving you the Holy Spirit, whom he promised long ago. The Spirit is God's guarantee that he will give us the inheritance he promised and that he has purchased us to be his own people.

—*Ephesians 1:13-14, NLT*

Reflect

What helps you believe wholeheartedly in the goodness of God?

Have you experienced things that have secured your belief in the Holy Spirit's constant presence?

Has it been hard for you to believe in a promise God has given? Why?

Thanks Be to God

Highlights

Return to your rest, O my soul,
For the LORD has dealt bountifully with you.
—Psalm 116:7, NKJV

Ponder
— REST —

Rest isn't a given in this hurried world, but for our spiritual and physical well-being, it's a necessity. God wants us to enjoy rest. Through the companionship of the Holy Spirit, we have what the world cannot give. When our spirit trusts God, our soul rests in the Lord, and our body settles into the relaxation it needs. Rest comes by recalling all the times God has been faithful to us. Part of the Holy Spirit's ministry is to help us *think* about those miracles. Fixing our thoughts on the way God's hand moves in our life—from meeting an impossible financial need to bringing a bluebird across our path to putting His glory on display at sunrise—gives the constant assurance that *God is with us*. Anything weighing on our hearts and minds can be dissipated by letting the Holy Spirit help us do what Jesus said to do: *Come to Me, all you who labor and are heavy laden, and I will give you rest* (Matthew 11:28, NKJV).

Meditate

We've all heard the phrase *It's easier said than done.* Considering the pace of our lives today, that phrase certainly applies to the mandate we're given to rest. With the help of the Holy Spirit—our continual path to calm—it's possible to surrender the weight of our days to our Savior. Leaning into the confidence the Holy Spirit provides, we're sure to trust the power we have in Jesus, and soon recognize it's the *only* way we'll find true rest for our souls.

Guide Me

Teach Me

Take My yoke upon you and learn from Me, for I am gentle and lowly in heart, and you will find rest for your souls.
—Matthew 11:29, NKJV

Reflect

Where or when do you feel most at rest?

How can you ask the Holy Spirit to show you ways to put your mind and body at ease more often?

Our hearts rest when we please God and follow Jesus. The Holy Spirit gives us strength and wisdom to do those things. How has He helped you be more passionate about your relationship with God?

Thanks Be to God

Highlights

Now hope does not disappoint,
because the love of God has been poured out in our hearts
by the Holy Spirit who was given to us.
—Romans 5:5, NKJV

Ponder

— HOPE —

Hopes dashed by the harshness of life can throw us into a sea of discouragement. Think of the Holy Spirit as God's life raft. Among the crashing waves of thought that scream, "You've made too many mistakes," "Your choices have destroyed your chances," or "God's promises have timed out," our Comforter's voice rises to the surface. *The Lord will not forsake his people, for they are his prize* (Psalm 94:14, TLB); *I will not abandon you or leave you as orphans in the storm—I will come to you* (John 14:18, TLB); *Be of good courage, and He shall strengthen your heart, all you who hope in the Lord* (Psalm 31:24, NKJV). The Holy Spirit, also called the Paraclete, shores up our strength and courage to hold on to the unsinkable hope in every promise God has made. When the things we see are taking *long* to line up with what God promises to do, we know our hearts are being shaped and molded during this time. Hope lives in our determination to believe God *will not* let go of us. Even if it may feel like we're abandoned in an ocean of heartache, disappointment, and rejection, we can know *this*—God is *with* us, working *in* us, and preparing to do great things *through* us by the power of His redemptive love.

Meditate

Listening to the Holy Spirit, who speaks only truth, keeps our hope afloat through every test and trial. Without faith, we can't please God, and there is no faith without hope attached securely to it. *What is faith? It is the confident assurance that something we want is going to happen. It is the certainty that what we hope for is waiting for us, even though we cannot see it up ahead* (Hebrews 11:1, TLB).

Guide Me

Teach Me

Glory be to God, who by his mighty power at work within us is able to do far more than we would ever dare to ask or even dream of—infinitely beyond our highest prayers, desires, thoughts, or hopes.

—Ephesians 3:20, TLB

Reflect

What are you hoping for that you can only envision right now? How is the Holy Spirit helping you while you wait for God's best?

When you feel discouraged, what Scriptures fill your heart and mind?

The Holy Spirit is a friend who encourages you. How do you actively listen and allow Him to lift you when you begin to lose hope?

Thanks Be to God

Highlights

The Lord is my fort where I can enter and be safe.
—Psalm 18:2, TLB

Week of: ___________

Ponder

— ENTER —

Where the presence of God dwells there is fullness of joy. The Holy Spirit enters into the center of our being, which means the truest joy is within us at all times. We then can enter into the presence of God and choose the joy of the Lord over doubt, self-pity, isolation, and regret. We can decide to embody the joy of the Lord in the midst of disappointing circumstances, bad days, unfair treatment from others, and the unanswered questions we have for God. Happiness is a feeling, but joy is a choice, rooted in a deeper sense of contentment and purpose. The Holy Spirit is the indwelling of every spiritual blessing we have in Christ—the grace to forgive, the strength to persevere, the courage to trust, and the willingness to enter God's courts with praise at all times and no matter what. Rejoicing is ours by the power of the Holy Spirit. God inhabits our praise, and joy saturates it. *Wisdom and truth will enter the very center of your being, filling your life with joy* (Proverbs 2:10, TLB). Truth and wisdom come to us when we trust God and let the Holy Spirit guide us on the path of righteousness. That path is where we are safe, content, thankful, and filled with the joy that draws the world to God.

Meditate

Joy acts differently than happiness—and the light of God's joy outshines our fleeting emotions. When we enter into and maintain a mindset of thankfulness and praise, we exude a joy that reflects the goodness of God. It's irresistible. It changes us, sets our countenance aglow, and attracts those who are seeking God, the giver of every good and perfect gift.

Guide Me

Teach Me

Go through his open gates with great thanksgiving; enter his courts with praise. Give thanks to him and bless his name.

—Psalm 100:4, TLB

Reflect

How do you feel changed when you enter into God's presence through thankfulness and praise?

The Holy Spirit is an abiding force of everything good that God is and gives. Record a recent time when it was difficult for you to cling to the Holy Spirit, trust God, and enter into joy.

In what areas of your life has the Holy Spirit invited you to enter into God's safety, protected from harm?

Thanks Be to God

Highlights

For now we see in a mirror, dimly, but then face to face.
Now I know in part, but then I shall know
just as I also am known.
—1 Corinthians 13:12, NKJV

Ponder

— ALIGN —

We won't always understand the reasons for the decisions God makes for our life, and we may not see all the rewards of trusting Him on this side of Heaven. The Holy Spirit is here to strengthen our trust muscles and continually remind us that seeing others through the lens of God's love is what matters most. When we are in tune with the Spirit of God, we see needs and speak timely words. *A word fitly spoken is like apples of gold in settings of silver* (Proverbs 25:11, NKJV). When we give the Holy Spirit control of our thoughts, we focus on doing good. *Let your light shine before men, that they may see your good works and glorify your Father in heaven* (Matthew 5:16, NKJV). When our words and actions are prompted by the Holy Spirit, others feel seen by God, the One who loves them wholly and without condition. The Spirit of God conveys things we cannot know about those who cross our paths or come into our lives. That's why prayerfully communicating and closely listening are invaluable disciplines in our relationship with the Holy Spirit—and we can sharpen both with daily practice.

Meditate

When we meet our heavenly Father, we will see clearly why His ways and purposes are far above our own. The gift of the Holy Spirit is a remarkable kindness from God to us, as His abiding presence provides everything we need to live a life that glorifies God. Not only does the Holy Spirit bring the truth of God's Word to our remembrance, but also He teaches us the beauty of following it.

Guide Me

Teach Me

Blessed are the pure in heart, For they shall see God.
—Matthew 5:8, NKJV

Reflect

When have you experienced a profound word spoken into your life when it was hard for you to see God?

How has the Holy Spirit helped you regain or deepen your trust in God's choices?

Do you feel you're hearing the Holy Spirit more clearly than you have before? What has helped you in your discipline to listen closely?

Thanks Be to God

Highlights

When the Holy Spirit has come upon you,
you will receive power to testify about me with great effect.
—*Acts 1:8, TLB*

Ponder

— STRENGTHEN —

Our spiritual strength is the most important part of our well-being. The Holy Spirit is the one we count on to make us strong from the inside out. He keeps us on the treadmill of truth. He emboldens us to speak about Jesus. The Spirit encourages our obedience to God. And He teaches us how to live according to our Creator's guidelines. *Bodily exercise is all right, but spiritual exercise is much more important and is a tonic for all you do. So exercise yourself spiritually, and practice being a better Christian because that will help you not only now in this life, but in the next life too* (1 Timothy 4:8, TLB). Practicing a daily, ongoing prayer life invites the Holy Spirit to be involved in the building up of our faith, the renewing of our mind, and the strengthening of our spirit. His purpose is to be our dependable friend, the Paraclete cheering us on to the finish line—the one alongside us in our time of need. *By our faith . . . the Holy Spirit helps us with our daily problems and in our praying. For we don't even know what we should pray for nor how to pray as we should, but the Holy Spirit prays for us with such feeling that it cannot be expressed in words. And the Father who knows all hearts knows, of course, what the Spirit is saying as he pleads for us in harmony with God's own will* (Romans 8:26–27, TLB). God's perfect will for our life is the Holy Spirit's standing prayer request—and the Father is faithful to answer it.

Meditate

Our strength is in God and the faithful, formidable work of the Holy Spirit within us. When we step into a day full of impossible expectations, He's not only our prayer partner, He's also the assurance that the will of God is our prevailing request. When our physical, mental, and spiritual tanks feel empty at the end of a day, He's our Strengthener and Standby, ready to equip us with ability, energy, and might.

Guide Me

Teach Me

When I think of the wisdom and scope of his plan,
I fall down on my knees and pray to the Father . . . that out of his glorious, unlimited resources he will give you the mighty inner strengthening of his Holy Spirit.

—Paul, as recorded in Ephesians 3:14–16, TLB

Reflect

The Father's resources are "glorious and unlimited." The Holy Spirit quickens them in our innermost being. What do you need from God most right now?

Is there an area in life where you feel spiritually weak? Write a prayer asking the Holy Spirit for strength to open your heart to God in a deeper way.

Giving our cares to God is a way to renew our strength and keep our eyes on opportunities He puts in front of us to love and serve others. What do you need to let go of to clear your spiritual vision?

Thanks Be to God

Highlights

Do you not know that your body is the temple of the Holy Spirit who is in you, whom you have from God, and you are not your own?
—1 Corinthians 6:19, NKJV

Ponder

— DWELL —

How often are we able to simply be still—as a temple—where the Holy Spirit dwells? The stillness creates calm, and the quietness nurtures a sweet sense of communion—a rare commodity in our lives today. Our routines are filled with demands and screens. The to-dos we feel compelled to complete are in a constant tug-of-war with our need to slow down and prioritize our relationship with the Spirit of God. And yet, time and again, His Word urges us not to be weighed down by the cares of this world. The Holy Spirit, if we are listening, reminds us of what Jesus said: *Come to me and I will give you rest—all of you who work so hard beneath a heavy yoke. Wear my yoke—for it fits perfectly—and let me teach you; for I am gentle and humble, and you shall find rest for your souls; for I give you only the light burdens* (Matthew 11:28–30, TLB). His commands are in agreement with the desire to teach us surrender. Laying down our choices, the obligations we commit to, even the time we volunteer—*everything*—is to choose God's lead. Grace will be sufficient when God is in control. We will have the time to sit, be still, and let the Holy Spirit refresh and lead us in ways He knows will make an eternal impact.

Meditate

The pace and race of this world can make being still feel unproductive. This thinking is at odds with our spiritual health. Running from one goal to the next, achieving one success after another, and filling our days with movement from beginning to end, serve only to exhaust every part of our being. God's plan is rooted in Jesus Christ and the wisdom of the Holy Spirit, given to us for the purpose of glorifying Him, serving others well, and affecting eternity.

Guide Me

Teach Me

Hold fast the pattern of sound words which you have heard from me, in faith and love which are in Christ Jesus. That good thing which was committed to you, keep by the Holy Spirit who dwells in us.
—2 Timothy 1:13–14, NKJV

Reflect

Make a plan for being more deliberate about sitting still, clearing your mind, and spending time with the Holy Spirit.

When you carve out time to sit quietly, how do you feel in your spirit?

At what times of the day do you feel more receptive to the inner voice of the Holy Spirit? Why is that?

Thanks Be to God

Highlights

Walk by the Spirit,
and you will not gratify the desires of the flesh.
For the flesh desires what is contrary to the Spirit,
and the Spirit what is contrary to the flesh.
—Galatians 5:16–17, NIV

Ponder

— LEARN —

As children of God and believers in Christ, following the Holy Spirit sets us on a path of lifelong learning. We learn from Jesus, our perfect example, who walked in the Spirit without pause and in complete oneness with His Father. We learn from every word our Savior spoke and every lesson He taught. While we won't attain perfection in this life, we can aspire to be more like Jesus every day through the presence and power of the Holy Spirit. Learning from Him is a gift and privilege we should never take for granted. *God sent the Holy Spirit to us. The power of God is living on the inside of us.* These are truths we should repeat every morning when we open our eyes. What we learn from the repetition is that *trusting* those words will open our spiritual eyes. Believing them wholeheartedly will enable us to see God's will more clearly and follow it more closely. Our flesh wants its own way and, without check, will insist on getting it. The Holy Spirit gives us the desire and strength to stand against worldly temptations and what is contrary to God's plan for us. In winning the battle, we learn that the Holy Spirit leads us into the most abundant, fulfilling life we could ever hope for.

Meditate

It is said that we should learn something new every day to stimulate our brain, boost our memory, and keep our mind sharp. It's even more beneficial for us to open our hearts and seek to learn from the Holy Spirit every day. He is the *voice of God* in our life! If we could come to the full realization of the amazing gift we've been given in the Holy Spirit, our life would be such a beacon of God's love and joy, no measure of darkness in this world could dim it.

Guide Me

Teach Me

The Advocate, the Holy Spirit, whom the Father will send in my name, will teach you all things and will remind you of everything I have said to you.

—John 14:26, NIV

Reflect

How do you learn best—by reading, listening, or experiencing? How might you depend on the Holy Spirit to teach you?

How do you distinguish between your own thoughts and feelings versus the Holy Spirit's guidance?

How has the Holy Spirit helped you stand against the desires of the flesh?

Thanks Be to God

Highlights

Glory in the Lord; O worshipers of God, rejoice.
Search for him and for his strength, and keep on searching!
—Psalm 105:3–4, TLB

Ponder
— SEARCH —

God's great power in helping us live a fulfilling life—abundant in love, joy, peace, patience, kindness, and self-control—comes from the Holy Spirit. The power that raised Jesus from death to life is active and dwelling within us. The awe of the Resurrection powerfully instills divine joy and a supernatural desire to love God by reflecting Him in all we do. When we allow the Holy Spirit to guide us, we have a divine searchlight directing our hearts to the people and places that need God's love. Our lives become a beacon shining out into a dark world with the Holy Spirit in the lead and love in control. We will know we're following the Holy Spirit when the fruit produced in our lives brings nourishment to the lives of others. Love does that. Joy does that. Forgiveness, grace, and kindness produce on behalf of God's Kingdom. Every good and perfect gift our Father gives—and others search for—will be found in us by way of the Holy Spirit.

Meditate

The Holy Spirit thrives when we seek Him and search to understand God's Word. Our souls are happiest when we know and live in the center of God's will. *Happy are all who search for God and always do his will* (Psalm 119:2, TLB). This world offers *nothing comparable* to serving God with our whole being; with the Spirit we are supercharged to love others out of deep compassion. A life filled with happiness is one filled with love—for God and for *every* person He created.

Guide Me

Teach Me

Every good gift and perfect gift is from above, and comes down from the Father of lights, with whom there is no variation or shadow of turning.

—James 1:17, NKJV

Reflect

When you study God's Word, how is your life of love shaped or changed? How does the Holy Spirit give you a renewed understanding and perspective?

When do you feel happiest?

A continual search for wisdom in God's Word and through our relationship with the Holy Spirit is vital to our spiritual maturity. How do you best retain the wisdom you gain? Use this journal to record your prayers and what the Holy Spirit says to you.

Thanks Be to God

Highlights

Let us not grow weary while doing good,
for in due season we shall reap
if we do not lose heart.
—Galatians 6:9, NKJV

Ponder

— GIVE —

A life of generosity is a blessed one. When we constantly listen to the Holy Spirit for ways to give and bless others, we crowd out thoughts that turn inward. We deny the tendencies of self-centered thinking and look outward to the needs around us. God will bring the seeking hearts, and the Holy Spirit will tell us how best to serve them. Our deepest desires should be anchored in giving. We are here only briefly in light of eternity, and every moment, day, and opportunity matters more than we know. The Holy Spirit knows all things and He sees every heart. It's the greatest reason for fostering an intimate relationship with Him. Being able to hear the Holy Spirit so clearly that we don't miss a single chance to give God's love away should be our highest goal. Love is the force capable of changing the world in ways the Spirit of God knows and sees, and in giving it, we are changed, too. We are transformed into someone who mirrors the character of God, for the purpose of reflecting who He truly is to a perishing world. A life marked by generous giving relays the message of a God who cares about us more than we can fathom.

Meditate

If we could see the harvest made possible by our giving without hesitation *every time* the Holy Spirit prompts us, our humbled hearts would break. God blesses us to be a blessing to others, and our heart and hand should open as freely and compassionately as our Father's. Giving our time, resources, talents, and energy can collectively reveal the glory of God in every corner of our world.

Guide Me

Teach Me

Don't grieve God. Don't break his heart. His Holy Spirit, moving and breathing in you, is the most intimate part of your life, making you fit for himself. Don't take such a gift for granted.

—*Ephesians 4:30, MSG*

Reflect

In what ways has God blessed your life and allowed you to be a blessing to others?

How do you receive or hear prompts from the Holy Spirit?

What different opportunities have opened up to you as you grow closer to the Holy Spirit?

Thanks Be to God

Highlights

Whatever things you ask in prayer,
believing, you will receive.
—Matthew 21:22, NKJV

Week of: ___________

Ponder

— RECEIVE —

The moment we accept Jesus Christ as our Savior, the Holy Spirit is ours to receive—and the power of Heaven comes with Him. Before Jesus ascended to Heaven, He explained to the disciples that upon His return to the right hand of His Father, the Holy Spirit was on His way to them. *When the Advocate comes, whom I will send to you from the Father—the Spirit of truth who goes out from the Father—he will testify about me* (John 15:26, NIV). Our friend, advocate, comforter, and indwelling prayer partner is here with us at all times. The Holy Spirit doesn't sleep, and He never leaves. He doesn't step away, even when we disappoint Him. He wants what is best for us with the same passion God does, and He's ready at all times to fight on our behalf. Our responsibility is to *listen*—to hear His voice over the taunts, temptations, and tales of the enemy. Both the enemy and God's Spirit vie for our undivided attention. But the more we listen to the Holy Spirit, receive His wisdom, and follow His direction, the clearer His voice becomes in our everyday life. Our dependence deepens, our trust grows, and we learn how important the Holy Spirit is in our living a life fully committed to God.

Meditate

The apostle Paul depended on the directives of the Holy Spirit—and he perfected his listening skills. In Acts 20:22–24, while saying goodbye to leaders in the church, Paul told them, "The Holy Spirit has let me know repeatedly and clearly that there are hard times and imprisonment ahead." We should aspire to hearing from the Spirit as clearly and as often as possible. And continue as Paul does, stating, *I consider my life worth nothing to me; my only aim is to finish the race and complete the task the Lord Jesus has given me—the task of testifying to the good news of God's grace* (NIV).

Guide Me

Teach Me

He who believes in Me, as the Scripture has said, out of his heart will flow rivers of living water. But this He spoke concerning the Spirit, whom those believing in Him would receive.
—John 7:38–39, NKJV

Reflect

What is your immediate response when you receive something you were believing God for?

Write a prayer of thanksgiving from your heart to His.

When the Holy Spirit directs you to do something, what thoughts occur when you doubt His voice?

Thanks Be to God

Highlights

Create in me a clean heart, O God,
and renew a steadfast spirit within me.
—Psalm 51:10, NKJV

Ponder

— RENEW —

It is through the sacrificial work of our Savior and His glorification that we have the wonderful gift of the Holy Spirit in our lives. The Spirit is *always* for us. He helps us run our race of faith with confidence and a renewed anticipation every day for what God is doing. We can wake up in the morning and boldly pronounce that God fills our lives with good things and renews our youth like the eagles! (Psalm 103:5). The Holy Spirit was sent by God to give us hope, to live our days on earth with a pure heart and a firm faith. God knew we would need the Holy Spirit to become more than conquerors in this life. The world is a broken and dark place, but we carry a light that cannot be dimmed. How it remains bright is not our burden, but the Holy Spirit's torch to bear. He will not fail. He ushers every single word from the promises of God to our hearts and minds. He takes *every* promise to the Father in prayer, holding it up to be fulfilled on our behalf; and in the name of Jesus, it *will* be.

Meditate

We have a daily assignment from our Father: *Do not be conformed to this world, but be transformed by the renewing of your mind, that you may prove what is that good and acceptable and perfect will of God* (Romans 12:2, NKJV). The Holy Spirit knows God's will inside and out, and He sees the direction we should go with clarity and wisdom (1 Corinthians 2:6–16). Following the Spirit closely renews our faith and sustains our hope—inviting the peace of God to rule our days.

Guide Me

Teach Me

According to His mercy He saved us, through the washing of regeneration and renewing of the Holy Spirit, whom He poured out on us abundantly through Jesus Christ our Savior.

—Titus 3:5–6, NKJV

Reflect

How do you make time to renew your mind every day?

What part of your faith walk do you feel needs growth and maturity?

Oftentimes, we try to appear spiritually perfect. How does that affect your peace? How might you need to repent and ask for God's mercy?

Thanks Be to God

Highlights

You must learn to know God better
and discover what he wants you to do.
—2 Peter 1:5b, TLB

Week of: ___________

Ponder

— DISCOVER —

If we're pursuing a God-glorifying life of purpose and meaning, the Holy Spirit is the one to help us discover it. God's plan for us unfolds through the infallible guidance of the Holy Spirit. Everything the Holy Spirit says lines up with God's truth, and everything worth having rests on its foundation. We're able to give gentle responses when we're angry. We're able to be patient and kind when we're tired. Our joy will not wane on days when one too many things go wrong. The world sees all the things the Spirit of God produces in us. In time, we learn that the fulfillment of serving God is more satisfying than any worldly possession or success. Nothing matters more than changing someone's eternal course. Our greatest blessings come by looking outward—outside ourselves—and giving as the Holy Spirit leads. The *ways* to give are as vast as the heavens. Many times, opportunities for giving stand right in front of us. Deciding to pay attention begins with every sunrise and a simple prayer: "Holy Spirit, show me where the love of God can fill a need today; give me the wisdom and courage to meet this calling." Not only do our days become more fulfilling, but also each day sets off a ripple effect with an eternal impact. Works of service motivated by God's love and inspired by the Holy Spirit make the most of our time and talents.

Meditate

The best possible life is ours to discover daily with the help of the Holy Spirit. A life spent loving God and loving people has no chance of becoming mundane or monotonous. The people and places that become part of our story are uniquely designed by our Creator, and the Holy Spirit is our "in-house manager."

Guide Me

Teach Me

God is not unjust to forget your work and labor of love which you have shown toward His name.

—Hebrews 6:10, NKJV

Reflect

Has God opened a door of giving or serving that you didn't expect? Can you trace the steps the Holy Spirit had you take to get there?

What have you discovered about your relationship with the Holy Spirit that blesses you most?

What has the Holy Spirit laid on your heart that you haven't pursued?

Thanks Be to God

Highlights

God has not given us a spirit of fear,
but of power and of love and of a sound mind.
—2 Timothy 1:7, NKJV

Week of: ___________

Ponder
— REPEAT —

There are phrases repeated throughout the Word of God that are worth noting. *Do not be afraid* is among them. The Holy Spirit is well aware that fear and anxiety are partners, and perils, for the children of God in this world. We have a number of weapons in our spiritual arsenal to choose from that are both alive and active: the boots of peace, the belt of truth, the breastplate of righteousness, the helmet of salvation, the shield of faith, and the sword of the Spirit! In addition to the spiritual armor, specific verses should be on repeat in our minds and hearts every day: *Be anxious for nothing, but in everything by prayer and supplication, with thanksgiving, let your requests be made known to God* (Philippians 4:6, NKJV); *Don't be anxious about tomorrow. God will take care of your tomorrow too. Live one day at a time* (Matthew 6:34, TLB); *Fear not, for I am with you. Do not be dismayed. I am your God. I will strengthen you; I will help you; I will uphold you with my victorious right hand* (Isaiah 41:10, TLB); *I am leaving you with a gift—peace of mind and heart! And the peace I give isn't fragile like the peace the world gives. So don't be troubled or afraid* (John 14:27, TLB). The gift of the Holy Spirit is ours for the purpose of bringing these peace-giving, spirit-nurturing words to our remembrance. All we need to do is tuck them into our memory bank and repeat them daily as we do any other health supplement. The benefits are 100 percent guaranteed.

Meditate

Remembering and repeating the truth of God's Word is the best way to keep our thoughts focused on good things, right things, and true things—all the things that have transformative power in our lives. *Whatever is true, whatever is noble, whatever is right, whatever is pure, whatever is lovely, whatever is admirable—if anything is excellent or praiseworthy—think about such things* (Philippians 4:8, NIV). The Holy Spirit comforts us in our emotional struggles, pours out healing oil to restore us, and strengthens us in our weaknesses.

Guide Me

Teach Me

He who is in you is greater than he who is in the world.
—1 John 4:4b, NKJV

Reflect

What are some of your fears or anxious thoughts that take you out of alignment with the Holy Spirit?

Write down a few Scripture passages that will help you combat fear.

How do you lean on the comfort of the Holy Spirit when you feel overwhelmed?

Thanks Be to God

Highlights

The wise learn by listening.
—*Proverbs 21:11, MSG*

Week of: ___________

Ponder

— LISTEN —

Distractions. They come from every angle. Psalm 131:2 says, *Surely I have calmed and quieted my soul* (NKJV). Quietness of heart is our work to do, with the Holy Spirit being a present and supportive companion who helps us. He knows that spiritual listening requires us to stifle the mental noise coming at us from every direction in our physical world. If we deny the Spirit—the stillness so vital to honing our listening skills—we feel increasingly agitated and impatient, and our days become void of peace. The Holy Spirit is one with the Prince of Peace. The Holy Spirit is one with the Father. We need to take time to listen *quietly*, and we need to form the habit of listening *closely* at all times. Both are necessary to our wholeness and well-being. We improve our Holy Spirit listening skills when we follow His voice often and consciously recognize how much He cares for us. Everything in our lives matters to Him. Leading us into God's best for our lives is His *constant* goal.

Meditate

There is no decision-making guidance more important than that of the Holy Spirit. As Jesus promises in John 16:13b, *He will guide you into all truth; for He will not speak on His own authority, but whatever He hears He will speak* (NKJV). When we accept the Holy Spirit as the divine gift He is, God's truth settles into our souls, and we can look forward to having strength, hope, and joy in every way. God will have our surrender, His Word will have control, and our hearts will desire righteousness through grace every day.

Guide Me

Teach Me

When we brought you the Good News, it was not just meaningless chatter to you; no, you listened with great interest. What we told you produced a powerful effect upon you, for the Holy Spirit gave you great and full assurance that what we said was true.

—1 Thessalonians 1:5, TLB

Reflect

How do you get away to quietly listen for God's voice and recharge?

What steps could you take to improve your ability to hear the Holy Spirit at all times?

What does it mean to "walk by the Spirit"?

Thanks Be to God

Highlights

Let each of you look out not only for his own interests, but also for the interests of others.

—*Philippians 2:4, NKJV*

Week of: ___________

Ponder

— LOOK —

The eternal impact of our life is in motion every day. We can be tempted to believe the lie that only certain days matter, that going through the motions is insignificant, or that the things we're doing in this season (which God ordained) have no lasting value. This is when we ask the Holy Spirit to strengthen us and renew our thinking—because *every* day in a life lived for God matters. *Look* for God's movement in your moments. *Look* for every chance to touch a life: inside your home, outside your home, in your neighborhood, while you run errands, on your walk, or while you shop. Treat *every* human interaction as a God-orchestrated opportunity to be a funnel for the unseen blessings of Heaven to pour into this world—through love, giving, kindness, patience, and forgiveness. Look out for others, let your eyes fill with tears of compassion, and reach out your hand to the needs you can meet. The spiritual scale that measures the success of our life is simply this: Everything we do as unto the Lord holds irrevocable weight in eternity. You are a priceless part of affecting this world for the glory of God through the everlasting work of love, and the Holy Spirit is your closest ally.

Meditate

God writes the beginning, middle, and end of our life's story. The Holy Spirit stands ready to help us live a life marked by trusting God and laying aside anything outside of His will. When we look to our Savior and the way He walked through this world, we see clearly how the Holy Spirit leads us—because our actions will become more and more like those of Jesus.

Guide Me

Teach Me

We do not look at the things which are seen, but at the things which are not seen. For the things which are seen are temporary, but the things which are not seen are eternal.
—2 Corinthians 4:18, NKJV

Reflect

Hebrews 12:1–2 says, "Let us lay aside every weight, and the sin which so easily ensnares us, and let us run with endurance the race that is set before us, looking unto Jesus, the Author and Finisher of our faith" (NKJV). Is there a weight you need to put aside?

At what times in your life have you relied on the Holy Spirit to provide endurance for the race?

What area of your life might you ask the Holy Spirit to illuminate with gratitude?

Thanks Be to God

Highlights

And here you yourself must be an example to them
of good deeds of every kind.
Let everything you do reflect your love of the truth.
—Titus 2:7, TLB

Ponder

— REFLECT —

The brightness, boldness, and beauty of our spiritual life are directly related to our being *continuously* receptive to the work of the Holy Spirit within us. He will use different ways to keep our feet on the path of God's purpose, which will keep God's love at the center of everything we do. The Spirit of God might prompt us through a conversation with a godly mentor, a good friend, a prayer partner, or a pastor's message. As we become more confident about hearing the Holy Spirit's direction and following without hesitation, we reflect God's glory more often and more clearly. That reflection not only changes the way we see ourselves, but also it changes the way people around us see God. Through our words, deeds, and actions, what do we reflect of the God who gives life and defines love? Grace that's greater than any wrong ever done? A hopeful path to their loving heavenly Father? A healing balm in the gift of the Holy Spirit, who will comfort them through every heartbreak, rejection, or disappointment? By being an example of God's miraculous power, we can inspire others to trust Him to do the same in their lives.

Meditate

Our lives are on constant display for the glory of God. Be inspired by those who received the Spirit on Pentecost. The apostle Peter recounts Jesus' words by quoting from the prophet Joel, *I will pour out my Holy Spirit upon all mankind, and your sons and daughters shall prophesy, and your young men shall see visions, and your old men shall dream dreams* (Acts 2:17, TLB). The actions we take, the words we speak, and our willingness to serve all reflect God's transforming love, guided by His Spirit.

Guide Me

Teach Me

We Christians have no veil over our faces; we can be mirrors that brightly reflect the glory of the Lord. And as the Spirit of the Lord works within us, we become more and more like him.
—2 Corinthians 3:18, TLB

Reflect

In what specific ways has the Holy Spirit led you to reflect God's character in your life?

It's sometimes challenging to reflect the love of God in tough situations, and even in close relationships. How has the Holy Spirit given you wisdom throughout these situations?

In what ways is the Holy Spirit nudging you to expand your scope of ministry or influence?

Thanks Be to God

Highlights

You are controlled by your new nature if you have the Spirit of God living in you.
—*Romans 8:9, TLB*

Ponder

— REMEMBER —

It's humbling to remember the way we were before surrendering to our "new nature"—and humility is a good thing. When the Holy Spirit moved in and brought the power of God with Him, our old nature was no longer welcome. *If anyone is in Christ, he is a new creation; old things have passed away; behold, all things have become new* (2 Corinthians 5:17, NKJV). Some of our unwelcome traits and habits left at once, some wanted to stick around, and some fell away as our relationship with the Holy Spirit matured. The war between our spirit and flesh ensued when we gave our life to Jesus Christ, and the battle will be ongoing until we leave this earth. One of the blessings of the Holy Spirit's ministry is echoing the words of our Savior while He was here: *With God all things are possible*; *Do not be afraid, only believe*; *In the world you will have tribulation; but be of good cheer, I have overcome the world* (Matthew 19:26, Mark 5:36, John 16:33, NKJV). Nothing apart from a life lived for Jesus can bring the security and *contagious* joy found in the Holy Spirit. When we anchor our spiritual well-being in His guidance, we remember how helpless we are without Him—and we rejoice in the assurance that we never have to.

Meditate

Wouldn't it be great to know that part of our giving to others is simply inspiring people to fall in love with Jesus? Seeing inexpressible joy we cannot contain speaks volumes to the Lord's provision and care. As the psalmist wrote, *And my soul shall be joyful in the LORD; It shall rejoice in His salvation* (Psalm 35:9, NKJV). The Holy Spirit illuminates true joy in us and reminds us to rejoice—our Savior has overcome *everything* that attempts to steal it.

Guide Me

Teach Me

And remember the words of the Lord Jesus, that He said, "It is more blessed to give than to receive."
—*Acts 20:35, NKJV*

Reflect

What are your favorite words spoken by Jesus? How are they a blessing to you?

How has God gifted you to inspire others?

How has the Holy Spirit freed you from your "old nature"?

Thanks Be to God

Highlights

Let us hold fast the confession of our hope
without wavering,
for He who promised is faithful.
—Hebrews 10:23, NKJV

Ponder

— HOLD —

The Holy Spirit cultivates the soil of our hearts. He encourages the Word of God to take hold while uprooting the weeds of sin from our lives. Once He begins the work of planting truth and growing a deeper love for God in us, He doesn't stop. Our newfound desires motivate us to hold on to the good things that begin *thriving* in us: peace that passes understanding, hope that won't fail, faith in what we can't see, and joy inexpressible—full of glory. Our wholeness is found solely in the person of Jesus Christ, and we no longer look to the world to satisfy our thirst for fulfillment. The Holy Spirit is in complete and constant agreement with every word God has spoken, bathing us in perfect light—where the fruit of the Spirit not only grows, but also flourishes. *You are a chosen generation, a royal priesthood, a holy nation, His own special people, that you may proclaim the praises of Him who called you out of darkness into His marvelous light* (1 Peter 2:9, NKJV). As we hold fast to the Holy Spirit, our lives bear fruit that does not perish, but rather becomes part of the great harvest in the fields of eternity.

Meditate

We hold closely the things we value most. Even from a materialistic standpoint, we keep the possessions that hold special meaning to us because they inspire remembrance of or thankfulness for the people and experiences in our lives. But nothing in this world should mean more to us than our relationship with God, the grace we're given through Jesus, or the gift we have in the Holy Spirit. Everything the Spirit of God does contributes to the blessed life Jesus came to give. Holding on to the Holy Spirit and nurturing our dependence on Him produces a harvest of divine fruit: love, joy, peace, patience, kindness, goodness, faithfulness, gentleness, and self-control.

Guide Me

Teach Me

But the fruit of the Spirit is love, joy, peace, longsuffering, kindness, goodness, faithfulness, gentleness, self-control. Against such there is no law.
—*Galatians 5:22–23, NKJV*

Reflect

What fruit of the Spirit comes naturally to you? What fruit may be difficult for you to produce?

In what ways have you grown spiritually in the last year?

What aspect of the Holy Spirit's friendship do you value most?

Thanks Be to God

Highlights

This is what I have asked of God for you: that you will be encouraged
and knit together by strong ties of love,
and that you will have the rich experience of knowing Christ
with real certainty and clear understanding.
—Colossians 2:2, TLB

Ponder

— ENCOURAGE —

God is truly wonderful. His sending the Holy Spirit to us is a gift we can never take for granted. Having a Comforter in our corner at all times is no small thing in a world growing colder every day. We couldn't serve God with strength, confidence, or *consistency* without Him. He's our *get-up-again* when we're knocked down by the pressures of this life. He's our *don't-give-up* when we're at our weakest. He's the one filling our thoughts with the life-giving, soul-encouraging Word of God when we feel unable to put our brokenness into prayer. Why do we lean on Him and learn these truths about Him? So we can draw near to God, receive encouragement, and offer the same encouragement to others. We can say with authority, "God will *never* give up on you; you can't hide from God's love for you; and you are *infinitely* valuable in the eyes of an infallible God." The Holy Spirit is our powerhouse of encouragement, given to us for the purpose of letting God's love flow through our changed, comforted heart into the hearts of others. There's no shortage of need in this world, and our suffering is wrought with divine reasons we won't always understand. But we rest assured that the Holy Spirit nurtures hope to get us through—and teaches us the way to lift others.

Meditate

The apostle Paul's prayers for the early church are worth putting on repeat when we need encouragement. Filled with the comfort and hope of the Holy Spirit, they remind us that God is the same loving Father who's as faithful now as He's been since the beginning of time. *We have kept on praying and asking God to help you understand what he wants you to do; asking him to make you wise about spiritual things; and asking that the way you live will always please the Lord and honor him* (Colossians 1:9b–10a, TLB). Not only does praying for others honor God through our care and compassion for the church, but also our hearts are encouraged throughout the time we spend with the Father.

Guide Me

Teach Me

What a wonderful God we have—he is the Father of our Lord Jesus Christ, the source of every mercy, and the one who so wonderfully comforts and strengthens us in our hardships and trials. And why does he do this? So that when others are troubled, needing our sympathy and encouragement, we can pass on to them this same help and comfort God has given us.

—2 Corinthians 1:3–4, TLB

Reflect

"May God our Father shower you with blessings and fill you with his great peace" (Colossians 1:2, TLB). Paul and Timothy prayed this simple prayer over the believers in the city of Colossae. How are you encouraged by these prayers that are inspired by the Holy Spirit?

How has the Holy Spirit encouraged you in the midst of a trial?

How have you encouraged someone experiencing their own trial?

Thanks Be to God

Highlights

Pray all the time. Ask God for anything in line with the Holy Spirit's wishes.
—*Ephesians 6:18a, TLB*

Week of: ___________

Ponder
— PRAY —

The Holy Spirit prays for us and knows exactly what we need. He sees the whole picture and *pleads for us in harmony with God's own will* (Romans 8:27b, TLB). We are on the receiving end of *every good thing* God gives when we believe. Not only does the Holy Spirit pray for us, but He also shores up the faith we need to see God's Word come to pass in our life. What we have in our court is *unstoppable*: an Almighty Father who loves us perfectly, a Savior who became our perfect sacrifice, and the Holy Spirit, who guides us into God's perfect will. Our prayers and the intercessory prayers of the Holy Spirit join forces to ring through the heavens on our behalf. Those prayers enter the throne room and meet God's grace. *Let us therefore come boldly to the throne of grace, that we may obtain mercy and find grace to help in time of need* (Hebrews 4:16, NKJV). We can pray, firmly believe, and see God move in our lives by the power of the Holy Spirit. A thankful and humble heart is the best company for every prayer we send—and we can wait in hopeful expectation for the outcome that brings God all the glory.

Meditate

Our faith in Jesus Christ is our righteousness, and the Holy Spirit empowers us to live a life that is pleasing to God. We would fail exceedingly without Him. Every day, we can be deeply grateful for the gift of the Holy Spirit, His prayer covering, and the solace He gives. God is *so* good, and the indwelling of the Holy Spirit is a confirming, continual reflection of that goodness.

Guide Me

Teach Me

The Spirit also helps us in our weaknesses. For we do not know what we should pray for as we ought, but the Spirit Himself makes intercession for us with groanings which cannot be uttered. Now He who searches the hearts knows what the mind of the Spirit is, because He makes intercession for the saints according to the will of God.

—Romans 8:26–27, NKJV

Reflect

How are you encouraged to know the Holy Spirit prays for you?

Praying invites peace into the deepest parts of us, even when we don't realize it. Take notes about the pattern of your prayer life.

The Holy Spirit teaches us to pray according to God's Word. What are your daily prayers from Scripture? How do you personalize them?

Thanks Be to God

Highlights

So get rid of all that is wrong in your life, both inside and outside,
and humbly be glad for the wonderful message we have received,
for it is able to save our souls as it takes hold of our hearts.
—James 1:21, TLB

Week of: ___________

Ponder

— COMMUNE —

The apostle John gave us some guidance in the beginning of the book of Revelation, also called the Revelation of Jesus Christ. *I was in the Spirit on the Lord's Day, and I heard behind me a loud voice, as of a trumpet, saying, I am the Alpha and the Omega, the First and the Last . . .* (Revelation 1:10–11a, NKJV). While John was in the Spirit, he heard the voice. That's the voice we want guiding us every day of our lives. Spending time in the presence of the Holy Spirit ushers in a sweet time of communion with our heavenly Father. It clears our minds and opens our hearts to the voice of our Savior, who is the beginning of every good thing and the end of every fear and doubt. As the early church grew in number, *The believers learned how to walk in the fear of the Lord and in the comfort of the Holy Spirit* (Acts 9:31, TLB). These actions go together. When we walk in the comfort of the Holy Spirit, our reverence for God deepens, and we develop an unquenchable desire to do His will. God's will leads us to the life we long for—a life of divine fulfillment, steeped in peace and purpose. S*pend your time and energy in the exercise of keeping spiritually fit* (1 Timothy 4:7, TLB).

Meditate

In our minds' eye, we might see ourselves reacting the same way John did to seeing our Savior in the fulness of His glory. But we should never feel timid about spending time with the Holy Spirit and facing our majestic Savior with anything that weighs down our heart. We can be awestruck but not afraid . . . reverent but not reluctant to come close . . . overwhelmed by God's love but not hesitant to accept the mercy and grace it offers. When the Holy Spirit has given us a chance to be a blessing but we ignore His prompt, we often feel convicted within moments. When we choose not to seek His guidance or wisdom, we miss opportunities for God's power to work in mind-blowing ways, and we miss glorifying God in a greater capacity. Our heavenly Father has a purpose for each of us that we may not fully comprehend—or follow—on our own; we must yield and accept the help of the Holy Spirit. Be encouraged to respond to the Holy Spirit's leading more faithfully each day.

Guide Me

Teach Me

Christians are God's house—he lives in us!—if we keep up our courage firm to the end, and our joy and our trust in the Lord. And since Christ is so much superior, the Holy Spirit warns us to listen to him, to be careful to hear his voice today and not let our hearts become set against him.

—Hebrews 3:6–8a, TLB

Reflect

When we make time to commune with the Holy Spirit, we welcome an intimate, spiritual connection with the Blessed Trinity. How do these times bring you peace and contentment?

The Spirit of God will speak differently at times—sometimes in a still, small voice—and sometimes we might describe it as an "almost audible" voice. Can you think of times in your life when you've heard the Holy Spirit in a louder, clearer voice?

When have you ignored or pushed aside a prompt from the Holy Spirit and missed the chance to be a blessing?

Thanks Be to God

Highlights

The righteousness of God is revealed from faith to faith;
as it is written, "The just shall live by faith."
—Romans 1:17, NKJV

Ponder

— LIVE —

No weapon formed against us can prosper, and no plan God puts in motion can fail. The Holy Spirit makes certain that we who belong to Christ will see the faithfulness of God, will have the courage to live for God, and will know we are *loved* by God—with every breath and without condition. The possibility of having a pure heart and living a life that pleases God is ours by grace and the gift of the Holy Spirit. Life is hard, and suffering is a part of it. If we don't keep our eyes fixed on Jesus and our focus on the power of the Holy Spirit, we won't be able to keep our spiritual head above water. God chose us to be His, and with that choice He planned to use our lives for a higher purpose that glorifies Him. The Holy Spirit knows how that purpose will unfold. He knows where we are on our journey and why we're at a particular mile marker. He won't force us to follow Him—but everything in us should want to. His voice isn't loud and demanding, but kind and gentle. The Spirit of God desires to help us live the fullest life possible by filling us with the power of God.

Meditate

Life in Christ is one of *abundance* in the good things God gives. When we pay close attention, the Holy Spirit reveals every chance we have on our journey to allow the love of God to flow through us, and He renews the joy of our salvation along the way. Love and joy are blessings that sustain our strength for the race we run to win. They are the good things that mark our finish line with a light that endures. *Let us run with endurance the race that is set before us* (Hebrews 12:1, NKJV).

Guide Me

Teach Me

The Holy Spirit displays God's power through each of us as a means of helping the entire church.

—1 Corinthians 12:7, TLB

Reflect

How would you define an abundant life in Jesus?

What is the most fulfilling part of hearing and obeying the Holy Spirit's direction to share God's love?

Write a prayer that reflects your heart's desire for God's direction and presence in your life.

Thanks Be to God

Highlights

Commit your way to the Lord, Trust also in Him,
And He shall bring it to pass.
He shall bring forth your righteousness as the light,
And your justice as the noonday.
—Psalm 37:5–6, NKJV

Ponder

— COMMIT —

Spiritual maturity requires commitment and a consistent yielding to the Holy Spirit. He's here to teach us how to live a beautiful, light-filled life for the glory of God. When we determine to daily relinquish our self-centered tendencies and stay tuned in to what the Spirit of God is doing, we live out the story God wrote for us. We experience the power of God working in us. We discover there is no true joy and fulfillment without investing in a vibrant, thriving relationship with our pure and holy God. The payoff is that *everything* in our life gets better. Our human relationships become even more meaningful. There's an authenticity that flows naturally from us as a result of discovering our truest self, by being more intimately bound to our Creator. *You saw me before I was born and scheduled each day of my life before I began to breathe. Every day was recorded in your book!* (Psalm 139:16, TLB). When our spiritual wholeness becomes the priority, our love for God outgrows any pursuit of earthly possessions. We learn that busyness does not lead to happiness and accomplishment does not sustain joy. The Holy Spirit helps to transform our thinking through *truth*: *Godliness with contentment is great gain. For we brought nothing into this world, and it is certain we can carry nothing out* (1 Timothy 6:6–7, NKJV).

Meditate

Many programs, diets, opportunities, and pastimes in this world offer fulfillment, but fall flat on the follow-through. God keeps His promise of a purposeful and satisfying life—and it's powered by the Holy Spirit. Supernatural gifts have a staying power unlike anything the world can offer us—and they bring the fulfillment that has the power to sustain us. *He himself gives life and breath to everything, and satisfies every need there is* (Acts 17:25b, TLB).

Guide Me

Teach Me

Above all else, guard your affections.
For they influence everything else in your life.
—*Proverbs 4:23, TLB*

Reflect

Peace to guard our hearts and minds; strength in Christ for everything we face; constant care, even to our old age: Which of these promises blesses you most and why?

How has the Holy Spirit shown you God's faithfulness recently?

What contributes most to your commitment to God and His will: love, respect, awe, or appreciation? How does the Holy Spirit encourage your discipline of faith?

Thanks Be to God

Highlights

It's the Spirit of God
and his glory in you that brought you
to the notice of others.
—1 Peter 4:14, MSG

Week of: ___________

Ponder

— RADIATE —

What type of person inspires you? Is it someone you perceive as joyful and bubbly, who lifts the energy in a room just by being in it? Is it someone who exudes light from the inside out through their eyes, their smile, or their words? Is it the one who jumps at the chance to help you however they can and whenever you need assistance? The way God's love radiates from each of us is different, and the wonderful truth is *all* personalities are needed in a searching world. God uses the unique qualities He gave us to reach those who crave the water that quenches every thirst for unconditional love, genuine peace, unfailing hope, and the indwelling presence of a God-given Friend. The gift of the Holy Spirit is a promise almost too hard to believe for those who don't understand the unfathomable goodness of God. And though *we're* fully aware of the Holy Spirit's friendship, we can be forgetful about honoring Him at all times and with every decision. The Holy Spirit is the reason God's love is *noticeable* in us. And when we come across a person who is inwardly grasping for validation and worth, I pray we *listen well.* In that moment, the Holy Spirit is aware of their need, and has a God-directed answer to meet it. When we're listening and obedient, He'll use us to do it.

Meditate

Every time the brightness of Heaven breaches the darkness of this world through our lives and the work of the Holy Spirit, it should make us rejoice. *God has given each of us the ability to do certain things well* (Romans 12:6, TLB). *Serve the Lord enthusiastically. Be glad for all God is planning for you* (Romans 12:11b–12a, TLB). With the Holy Spirit giving us the power to serve God honorably, our response should be to do so energetically!

Guide Me

Teach Me

Those who are wise shall shine Like the brightness of the firmament,
And those who turn many to righteousness
Like the stars forever and ever.
—Daniel 12:3, NKJV

Reflect

In what ways does the love of Jesus radiate from you? How have others helped you see it?

What are your spiritual gifts (Romans 12)?

How have you been tempted to dim your light or "put your light under a bushel" and not shine for Christ?

Thanks Be to God

Highlights

God's blessings are given to us by faith, as a free gift.
—*Romans 4:16a, TLB*

Ponder

— BLESS —

If we are hearing and obeying the Holy Spirit, the blessings of God should move through our lives like a stream running down a mountainside. There's only one way for eternal blessings to flow—from the highest love in the universe to the depth of human hearts. God's infinite and unrelenting love moves freely and unobstructed through us into the life of a grieving friend, a helpless stranger, a neighbor battling illness, or a coworker going through a painful divorce. Loss comes to the lost as well as the saved, and the Comforter sees any heartache with the compassion of God. The Holy Spirit *knows* what will make the biggest difference in every soul crying out to God in silent suffering. Each of us is the human link that animates the difference-making love of God in the world. Heeding the instruction of the Holy Spirit enables us to become the hands and feet of Christ. The smallest drop of perfect love can heal the deepest wound, soothe the sharpest pain, and warm the coldest heart. When put into practice, God's love can heal our world.

Meditate

When we listen to the Holy Spirit, we hold the power of God and loose it through the love we give. A *practiced listener* is a force for good and a reflection of God. *Live and act in a way worthy of those who have been chosen for such wonderful blessings as these. Be humble and gentle. Be patient with each other, making allowance for each other's faults because of your love. Try always to be led along together by the Holy Spirit and so be at peace with one another* (Ephesians 4:1–3, TLB).

Guide Me

Teach Me

Blessed are all who hear the Word of God and put it into practice.

—Luke 11:28, TLB

Reflect

In what ways do you feel blessed by the Holy Spirit today?

In the world today, what moves your heart toward compassion? Write a prayer asking to be part of the solution to bless others in this circumstance.

When the Holy Spirit asks you to share God's love in a way that moves you out of your comfort zone, how do you respond? What acts of service challenge your courage?

Thanks Be to God

Highlights

Jesus replied, "Love the Lord your God with all your heart, soul, and mind." This is the first and greatest commandment. The second most important is similar: "Love your neighbor as much as you love yourself."

—Matthew 22:37–39, TLB

Week of: ___________

Ponder

— LOVE —

The motivation for every decision, desire, or deed directed by the Holy Spirit is love. Jesus tells us that *every* commandment from God hangs on the first two: love God and love your neighbor. The guidance of the Holy Spirit will never deviate from the definition of love. *Love suffers long and is kind; love does not envy; love does not parade itself, is not puffed up, does not behave rudely, does not seek its own, is not provoked, thinks no evil; does not rejoice in iniquity, but rejoices in the truth; bears all things, believes all things, hopes all things, endures all things. Love never fails* (1 Corinthians 13:4–8a, NKJV). These verses could serve as an instruction booklet for following the Holy Spirit. The choices He makes for us will accomplish the *most* good for the *most* people—because that's what love does. Love is the crucial framework for serving God in whatever we do, wherever we go, and for the good of whoever we meet. Loving God with all our heart, soul, and mind is the starting line. We need time in prayer and the Word to prepare for any love-powered action we take—which is *everything* we do for the glory of God.

Meditate

God's love is a floodlight in this world. It illuminates every act the Holy Spirit directs and every deed done for the glory of God. We are blessed to be a small part of the warmth it creates and the impact it makes. By receiving the gift of the Holy Spirit, we realize the amazing impact we can have on the lives of others through His continual guidance. To bring a glimpse of unconditional love to someone who may not know their infinite worth in God's sight is the most fulfilling work we will do on this earth. We are blessed to be a blessing!

Guide Me

Teach Me

For you are the Fountain of life; our light is from your light. Pour out your unfailing love on those who know you! Never stop giving your blessings to those who long to do your will.

—Psalm 36:9–10, TLB

Reflect

How do you invest in your relationship with God?

How has your deepening love for God and what He's done in your life contribute to your desire to share His love with others?

What do you think it means to love God with all your strength?

Thanks Be to God

Highlights

As the deer pants for water, so I long for you, O God.
—Psalm 42:1, TLB

Week of: ___________

Ponder

— YEARN —

Not only should we gratefully receive the gift of the Holy Spirit, but also we should yearn to *continuously* follow His wise counsel. There are times when God provides confirmation that we're hearing the Holy Spirit clearly, and this is a humbling, wonderful thing. God is gracious. He understands that revealing what our Spirit-led actions have done is a faith booster and a blessing. We're also encouraged to do more *listening*, followed by *doing*. If we fall into a habit of being spiritually lazy, whisking through our days and weeks without *actively* involving the Holy Spirit, an underlying sadness sets in. There's sorrow that comes with dismissing the Holy Spirit's presence and power in our lives. Neglecting a God-given gift is no small thing. Instead of being guided into God's perfect will and taking advantage of the built-in wisdom for life, we glide through hectic days with little thought of consequence. For a while, we might buy the deception that things are going well enough. There is never a good time to neglect the Holy Spirit. We should rely on Him so heavily that ignoring Him gives us an immediate sense that something isn't right. Communicating with Him is our constant life support from a spiritual standpoint. The Holy Spirit is the proclamation within us that we belong to Christ, we're children of God, and we're on our way to an eternity in His glorious presence.

Meditate

The Holy Spirit identifies each of us in the spiritual realm as a child of God, redeemed by the perfect sacrifice of Jesus Christ. Chosen, loved, and adopted into God's family, we are empowered by the Holy Spirit to live out this true and eternal identity. God looks at us and knows we're on our way to Him—and that makes His heart rejoice.

Guide Me

Teach Me

Do not cast me away from Your presence, And do not take Your Holy Spirit from me. Restore to me the joy of Your salvation, And uphold me by Your generous Spirit.
—*Psalm 51:11–12, NKJV*

Reflect

Have you ever neglected the Holy Spirit for a period of time, believing you could go it alone? Record thoughts and feelings about that time in your life.

How vital is the Holy Spirit in your everyday life?

Think of a time when God revealed how the Holy Spirit used you to be a blessing. How did that interaction encourage you?

Thanks Be to God

Highlights

The wisdom that comes from heaven is first of all pure and
full of quiet gentleness. Then it is peace-loving and courteous.
It allows discussion and is willing to yield to others;
it is full of mercy and good deeds.
It is wholehearted and straightforward and sincere.
—James 3:17, TLB

Ponder

— UNDERSTAND —

Those who haven't received the gift of the Holy Spirit through salvation in Jesus Christ cannot understand spiritual truths. *The natural man does not receive the things of the Spirit of God, for they are foolishness to him; nor can he know them, because they are spiritually discerned* (1 Corinthians 2:14, NKJV). As believers, we can translate an important truth to unbelievers by the power of *agape* love and the gentle, humble guidance of the Holy Spirit. Love needs no explanation and doesn't require a spiritually mature discourse to be understood. Love needs *willing participants*. Love needs the body of Christ to serve those in need with humility and gentleness. Love needs those who *do* have the Holy Spirit to listen with all our hearts and love with all our strength. Every other commandment God gives hinges on loving Him and loving our neighbor. When compassion is our highest goal, divisive behavior is overshadowed by perfect love. The need to prove others wrong falls away. Selfish pride fades into the background. When we walk in the light as He is in the light, the Father's perfect love can work miracles in a searching heart, a doubting mind, and a lost soul. Let's ask the Holy Spirit to give us wisdom from Heaven today to change someone's tomorrow for the better through the pure, gentle power of love.

Meditate

Peace is a trait of heavenly wisdom. It's also the Holy Spirit's manner of guiding and showing us how to love others in a way that opens their hearts to the saving grace of Jesus Christ. Love leads to understanding through the miracle of salvation. God may choose us, and use us, to begin the process.

Guide Me

Teach Me

The God of our Lord Jesus Christ, the Father of glory . . . give to you the spirit of wisdom and revelation in the knowledge of Him, the eyes of your understanding being enlightened; that you may know what is the hope of His calling, what are the riches of the glory of His inheritance in the saints, and what is the exceeding greatness of His power toward us who believe, according to the working of His mighty power.

—*Ephesians 1:17–19, NKJV*

Reflect

From the following list, what characteristic of heavenly wisdom inspires you most?: Pure, peace-loving, gentle, submission, merciful, produces good fruit, impartial, sincere.

How do you ask God for wisdom and understanding when making a decision to serve?

The Holy Spirit can open our eyes to very simple acts of love every day, knowing their impact will be much greater than we can see. How do you stay alert to the needs around you?

Thanks Be to God

Highlight

Live and act in a way worthy of those who have been chosen for such wonderful blessings as these.

—Ephesians 4:1b, TLB

Ponder
— RESPOND —

The Holy Spirit won't prompt us to respond to every need we see, and He won't put us under obligation to offer our time and skills every time they are requested. Following the Spirit doesn't mean we go until we're exhausted, scrambling here and there in an attempt to prove our love for God or our value as a servant of God. If we find ourselves feeling stretched thin and drained empty of the grace we need to walk in peace, evaluation is in order. The Holy Spirit may ask us to step back, take time to refresh our minds and bodies, quiet ourselves before God, and simply rest. We have the power of God living within us, but nevertheless, we're on a human pilgrimage through this life. There is much to do for the Kingdom of God, but we must remain in the Vine (Jesus) and feed off of the Spirit as His branches. We shouldn't do what the Holy Spirit doesn't orchestrate. *O LORD, You have searched me and known me. You know my sitting down and my rising up; You understand my thought afar off. You comprehend my path and my lying down, And are acquainted with all my ways* (Psalm 139:1–3, NKJV). Some of the "no's" the Holy Spirit gives are for the purpose of holding our feet to the path God has for us. That's where we're needed most, where we can be the greatest blessing, and most importantly, where we might affect a life for eternity.

Meditate

Obeying God brings blessing—to our lives and to every life we touch. Immerse yourself in the study of God's Word, engage in consistent prayer, and practice your listening skills. Listening to the Holy Spirit holds our feet to the path paved by love's design. Jesus followed to the point of death—His destiny was the cross, His purpose was love, and His reason was *you*.

Guide Me

Teach Me

These laws of yours have been my source of joy and singing through all these years of my earthly pilgrimage. I obey them even at night and keep my thoughts, O Lord, on you. What a blessing this has been to me—to constantly obey.

—*Psalm 119:54–56, TLB*

Reflect

Have you felt tired from saying "yes" to others too often? When have you moved forward without the peaceful guidance of the Holy Spirit?

What personal checks could you put in place to slow down your decision making?

In what areas are you most thankful for the companionship of the Holy Spirit?

Thanks Be to God

Highlights

Most important of all,
continue to show deep love for one another,
for love makes up for many of your faults.
—1 Peter 4:8, TLB

Ponder
— CONTINUE —

As we continue our pursuit of a deeper relationship with the Holy Spirit, our spiritual eyes become sharper, while our responses to His guidance are quicker and more assured. The world is growing darker, and by the heartbreaking headlines we see, we're reminded on a daily basis of humanity's rejection of God's love. It can be difficult to believe our strides are making a difference. Some days we might feel too discouraged to continue, tempted to retreat and wait for Jesus to return. But we can't see the whole picture. We don't fully understand the magnitude of God's grace. Our continual and deliberate responses *must* be to love God most and reflect His love in a more grace-filled way to the people around us. We should feel compelled to choose joy over bitterness and grace over divisiveness. Unity is one of love's greatest strengths, and division is one of the *hardest* tactics of the enemy to conquer. If there's a single strategy the Holy Spirit knows perfectly, it's unity through love—by the compassion of God and the sacrifice of Jesus. Trusting that love never fails is how we pray our way forward in the face of insurmountable odds, knowing we need the miracle-working power of our merciful, loving God to beat them.

Meditate

As we continue to press on by faith in the God who is able to redeem and restore all things, we pray in agreement with the Holy Spirit that His perfect will be done—in our lives, in our choices, and in every act of love we put into the world. Our actions solidify—or dilute—the perfect love of the God we profess to serve. We are known by the fruit our life produces, fruit that can only become more desirable through a greater dependence on the Holy Spirit.

Guide Me

Teach Me

My Holy Spirit shall not leave them, and they shall want the good and hate the wrong—they and their children and their children's children forever.

—Isaiah 59:21, TLB

Reflect

How do you nurture your continually growing friendship with the Holy Spirit?

Whom do you struggle to love unconditionally? Write a prayer asking the Holy Spirit to lead you forward in this area.

God's will is found in His Word. As God's Word becomes more dominant in our lives, in our thinking, and in our feelings, the will of God becomes more prominent—replacing our own will. How confident are you about hearing the Holy Spirit in this process and why?

Thanks Be to God

Highlights

Clearly you are an epistle of Christ . . .
written not with ink but by the Spirit of the living God,
not on tablets of stone but on tablets of flesh, that is, of the heart.
—2 Corinthians 3:3, NKJV

Week of: ___________

Ponder

— SEE —

By the Spirit of God, we understand the Word of God in a way that helps us see His constant presence in our lives. Our spiritual eyes are opened. Because the Holy Spirit teaches us all things and reveals to us the wisdom in God's Word, we have a higher mandate to expose (and express) God's love to those who are hurting or lost. The Holy Spirit leads us to be careful and wise in our actions because the world is watching, and more than anything, we want our neighbors, friends, and family to see a magnificent, merciful Father. Since we are freely given the gifts of God, grace demands that we offer them freely to others. When the people around us see kindness in our actions and generosity from our hand, submersed in the joy of the Lord, we succeed in writing the goodness of God on the tablet of their hearts. That's how the enduring gifts of love make their way to eternal differences. By the Holy Spirit's vibrant, life-giving force within us, what the world sees in us inspires them to turn their focus from the act of love to Love Himself. We might facilitate God's heart-changing work by following the Holy Spirit, and we become a human link in the powerful chain of God's deepest desire that none perish but *all* come to repentance (2 Peter 3:9).

Meditate

It's an astounding privilege to be chosen to join God's work on earth. To be given the Holy Spirit as a guide is equally humbling. If we wake up every day in a manner of praise for all God has done, we open our hearts to doing all that *can* be done—for the glory of our Father, the good of our lives, and a lasting change in the lives of others.

Guide Me

Teach Me

Be careful how you act; these are difficult days. Don't be fools; be wise: make the most of every opportunity you have for doing good.
—Ephesians 5:15–16, TLB

Reflect

How do you make the most of simple opportunities to lend a hand or share God's love?

As your relationship with the Holy Spirit has grown, how have you been able to ask for direction and respond more quickly?

Can you think of a few ways the Holy Spirit has led you to share God's love this week?

Thanks Be to God

Highlights

In every battle you will need faith as your shield
to stop the fiery arrows aimed at you by Satan.
—Ephesians 6:16, TLB

Ponder

— STOP —

How do we keep the enemy from influencing our minds, which in turn affects everything else in our lives? We stop the thoughts that are driven by lies and replace them with the truth of God's Word. The Holy Spirit is a powerful defender of everything true, noble, just, pure, lovely, and praiseworthy. We get better at stopping negative thoughts by getting *really good* at listening to the Comforter's voice. Our faith is another line of defense that acts as a shield to stop thoughts aimed at our peace of mind. *Because of our faith, he has brought us into this place of highest privilege where we now stand, and we confidently and joyfully look forward to actually becoming all that God has had in mind for us to be* (Romans 5:2, TLB). One of the most effective ways to stop the lies of the enemy is to look forward, fixing our thoughts on what God is doing in us as we become more like Him. The Holy Spirit plays a powerful part in our transformation. When He speaks, He fills our hearts and minds with the will of God for our lives. As we listen and obey, we become all God has in mind for us to be—and by faith it's going to be better than we ever imagined it could be.

Meditate

The good things God has for us were planned before we were born. The sooner we stop the thoughts that run contrary to the place of high privilege we now stand in, the quicker we become all the Holy Spirit is helping us to be—a favored, blessed, confident, and joyful child of God. Thought-stopping is a practice worth perfecting, and it gives us the pause needed to bring every thought into the obedience of Christ. *For the weapons of our warfare are not carnal but mighty in God for pulling down strongholds, casting down arguments and every high thing that exalts itself against the knowledge of God, bringing every thought into captivity to the obedience of Christ* (2 Corinthians 10:4–5, NKJV).

Guide Me

Teach Me

Whatever things are true, whatever things are noble, whatever things are just, whatever things are pure, whatever things are lovely, whatever things are of good report, if there is any virtue and if there is anything praiseworthy—meditate on these things.

—Philippians 4:8, NKJV

Reflect

What Scriptures help you stop wrong thoughts and replace them with right and true ones?

Ask the Holy Spirit to help you meditate on God's goodness. What things come to mind?

Thinking about what God has done for you can strengthen and build your faith. What miracles from God's Word encourage you?

Thanks Be to God

Highlights

Do you not know that you are the temple of God
and that the Spirit of God dwells in you?
—1 Corinthians 3:16, NKJV

Ponder

— VISUALIZE —

Picture yourself as a dwelling place of God. He inhabits every part of your being and feels welcome there. Your thoughts surround Him, your heart allows Him access to every room and every hidden corner, and you feel good about Him seeing and hearing *everything* that enters through your eyes and ears. When you commit the operation of your dwelling place to Jesus Christ, God bestows the gift of the Holy Spirit—who, by God's eternal power, provides wisdom, comfort, counsel, and peace. The Holy Spirit moves into your innermost being as a teacher and friend. Every word He speaks is for the purpose of keeping your life blessed and the will of God in control. All the light emanating from you shines for the glory of God. Your dwelling place is whitewashed with forgiveness and filled wall-to-wall with hope. Imagine this is you, and every word and deed that goes out from you is wrapped in a love so pure that everyone it reaches is drawn to its source. This is how we build a constantly growing temple for God and live a life that's far greater in purpose than we ever thought possible.

Meditate

When we visualize being an actual dwelling place for the power of Heaven, our reverence for God escapes a fitting expression. Our gratefulness goes beyond words, and our highest praise is the only thing worth offering—for the mercy of God, the sacrifice of Jesus, and the gift of the Holy Spirit. Living a life that is made possible only by the *empowerment* of God's Spirit is the purest worship we can offer each day.

Guide Me

Teach Me

We who believe are carefully joined together with Christ as parts of a beautiful, constantly growing temple for God. And you also are joined with him and with each other by the Spirit and are part of this dwelling place of God.

—Ephesians 2:21–22, TLB

Reflect

When you think about all God has given you in order to live a blessed life, what is your prayer of thankfulness?

What do you appreciate most about the gift of the Holy Spirit?

How is your ministry to others shaped by the inspiration of the Holy Spirit?

Thanks Be to God

Highlights

Friendship with God is reserved
for those who reverence him.
—*Psalm 25:14a, TLB*

Ponder

— RESPECT —

We wouldn't think of deliberately hurting people we respect or quickly dismissing someone we love. In the same manner, our relationship with the Spirit of God is more important than any human relationship we have, and honoring the Holy Spirit is an irreplaceable aspect of living a holy life. We won't be able to manage our emotions, maintain our hope, or mirror our Savior without counting on the Holy Spirit to help us. When we fail to defer to Him (and we will), He is faithful to reveal the lesson in it and give us wisdom on the best way to handle the situation should it arise again. He teaches us continually for the sake of lovingly changing us into the truest version of ourselves—children of God. The Holy Spirit is worthy of our perpetual attention. He lives within us to strengthen our resolve against the devices of the enemy and to remind us of the weapon we have in God's Word to defeat every attack launched at us. The Spirit's leadership strategy is *peace*. We can depend on the Holy Spirit's faithful response, and if we don't feel peace about a thought or decision, we wait. *The reverence and fear of God are basic to all wisdom. Knowing God results in every other kind of understanding* (Proverbs 9:10, TLB). Opening our hearts and minds to understanding the will of God for our lives through the navigation of the Holy Spirit is the way to a peaceful, purposeful adventure.

Meditate

The conviction to please God in everything we do usually comes gradually, through a genuine, mature relationship with the Holy Spirit. Even the growing desire to *listen* to the Holy Spirit and reverence God in everything we do is a blessing. The process is both humbling and amazing, as we begin to fully realize the power that dwells inside us with every breath we take.

Guide Me

Teach Me

Be even more careful to do the good things that result from being saved, obeying God with deep reverence, shrinking back from all that might displease him.

—Philippians 2:12b, TLB

Reflect

The reverence of God is basic to all wisdom. How has the Holy Spirit changed your desires through the revelation He's given you?

How do you feel when you hear and follow the Holy Spirit? What result of your obedience confirms His divine wisdom?

In what ways has your love and reverence for God developed since you gave your life to Jesus?

Thanks Be to God

Highlights

May God's love and the Holy Spirit's friendship be yours.
—2 Corinthians 13:14b, TLB

Week of: ___________

Ponder

— BEFRIEND —

The fruit of our lives reflects our friendship with the Holy Spirit. Meaningful connections, loving reactions, encouraging conversations, and purpose in every human interaction all signal the divine friendship we have with Jesus and the power we've been given through His sacrifice. That power is received in the gift of the Holy Spirit, and it's essential to our victorious life on this earth. It's how we make a difference, how we make it through our trials, how we learn through every test, and how God generously gives us *everything* we need to know and serve Him well. The Holy Spirit widens our understanding, builds our trust, and deepens our desire for the things *God* wants for us. They're the best things. They're eternal things. The love we give, the joy we inspire, the kindness we show, and the friendships we nurture are the only things that will live beyond our walk through this world. Every day brings us a little closer to the end, and our steps feel like they swell with meaning and should be taken with intention. The Holy Spirit is our guide to putting each of our steps where they should be. He'll make certain we go where we should go, meet who we should meet, and shine the love of God on the path to eternity for every life we touch.

Meditate

Meditate on this for a moment today: *Christ has entered into heaven itself to appear now before God as our Friend* (Hebrews 9:24a, TLB). It's nearly breathtaking to believe this. We, who have done nothing to deserve His love, are befriended by the Savior of the world. And He bestowed the power of that friendship through the gift of the Holy Spirit. Truly, all things are possible if our faith is anchored in the God who gave both His Son and His Spirit.

Guide Me

Teach Me

I assure you of this: I, the Messiah, will publicly honor you in the presence of God's angels if you publicly acknowledge me here on earth as your Friend.

—Luke 12:8, TLB

Reflect

How does it bring you comfort to view the Holy Spirit as your friend?

In what ways could you further develop your friendship with Him?

Record a meaningful conversation with the Holy Spirit and look back on this entry to remember His active presence in your life.

Thanks Be to God

Highlights

Prayer Requests

Date

Praise

Repent

Acknowledge

Yearn

Answered Prayers

Date

Praise

Repent

Acknowledge

Yearn

Prayer Requests

Date

Praise

Repent

Acknowledge

Yearn

Answered Prayers

Date

Praise

Repent

Acknowledge

Yearn

Prayer Requests

Date

Praise

Repent

Acknowledge

Yearn

Answered Prayers

Date

Praise

Repent

Acknowledge

Yearn

ABOUT THE AUTHOR

Bonnie Rickner Jensen grew up with a father and mother who loved God and modeled His grace to their six children. She thinks of her dad as a "car ride" preacher who spent the countless road trips of her childhood teaching his children the truth of God's Word. She gave her life to Jesus when she was 12 years old. After graduating from Oak Harbor High School in northwest Ohio in 1980, she became a young wife and mother of three daughters.

Bonnie began her professional writing career at Hallmark Cards in their Christian division (DaySpring). She was promoted to Senior Writer after three years of employment. Her professional writing career has spanned 30 years. While employed at Hallmark, she began writing children's books through a partnership with HarperCollins Christian Publishing. Bonnie is the bestselling author behind the *Really Woolly* brand, with more than 1.6 million books sold, and the ECPA gold award-winning *Really Woolly Bedtime Prayers.*

Her three-book devotional series, *The Beach is Calling*, *The Campfire is Calling*, and *The Mountains are Calling*, consistently sells well and garners inspirational reviews, both publicly and through private messaging. *God in Every Moment* and *In This Together* are additional titles Bonnie has written for DaySpring. Publishers Bonnie has worked with include Barbour Publishing, DaySpring, Guideposts, Hachette Book Group, Hallmark, HarperCollins Christian Publishing, Paraclete Press, and Callisto Publishing.

ABOUT PARACLETE PRESS

Paraclete Press is the publishing arm of the Cape Cod Benedictine community, the Community of Jesus. Presenting a full expression of Christian belief and practice, we reflect the ecumenical charism of the Community and its dedication to sacred music, the fine arts, and the written word.

EXPLORE MORE PARACLETE PRESS RESOURCES ABOUT THE HOLY SPIRIT

40 Days with the Holy Spirit: Fresh Air for Every Day
by Jack Levison (ISBN: 978-1612616-384)

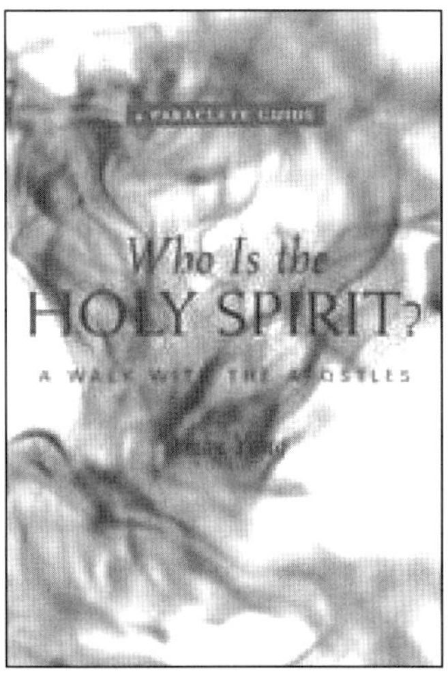

Who is the Holy Spirit? A Walk with the Apostles
by Amos Young (ISBN: 978-1557256-355)

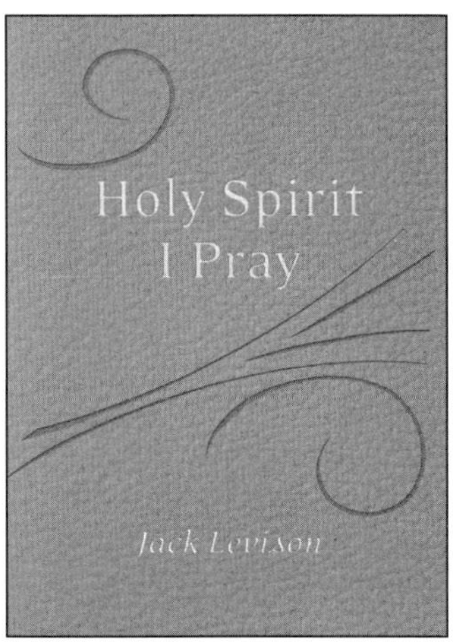

Holy Spirit, I Pray: Prayers for morning and nighttime, for discernment, and moments of crisis
by Jack Levison (ISBN: 978-1640602-250)